JOB INTERVIEV

Be Your Own Coa

JOB INTERVIEW SUCCESS

Be Your Own Coach

Jenny Rogers

Open University Press

Job Interview Success
Be Your Own Coach

Jenny Rogers

ISBN 13: 978-0-07-713018-3
ISBN 10: 0-07-713018-9

 **Professional**

Published by:
McGraw-Hill Publishing Company
Shoppenhangers Road, Maidenhead, Berkshire, England, SL6 2QL
Telephone: 44 (0) 1628 502500
Fax: 44 (0) 1628 770224
Website: www.mcgraw-hill.co.uk

British Library Cataloguing in Publication Data
A catalogue record of this book is available from the British Library.

McGraw-Hill books are great for training, as gifts, and for promotions. Please contact our corporate sales executive to discuss special quantity discounts or customisation to support your initiatives: b2b@mcgraw-hill.com.

Fictitious names or companies, products, people, characters and/or data that may be used herein (in case studies or in examples) are not intended to represent any real individual, company, product or event.

Printed in Great Britain by Bell and Bain Ltd, Glasgow.

The **McGraw·Hill** Companies

CONTENTS

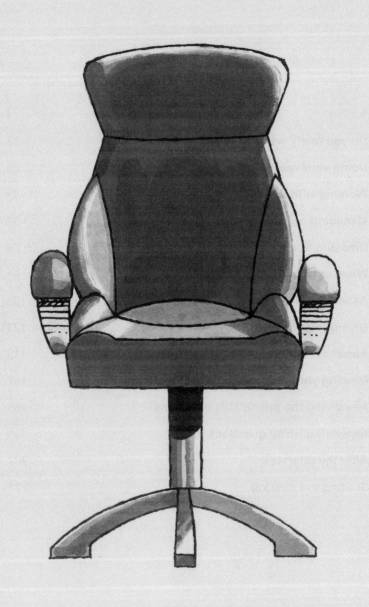

INTRODUCTION

Y ou will have come to this book because you are at a crossroads in your career and have been invited to an interview for a job. This is not an everyday event and it is a stressful one. I have coached many hundreds of people through their preparation for what could well be a life-changing experience, so I know all about the mixture of fear and excitement that most people typically bring to it.

You should read this book if

- You have been shortlisted many times but have failed to get an offer: this suggests that there is something seriously amiss with your interview technique.
- Redundancy is possible and you know you could be on the jobs market soon. It may seem a daunting prospect, especially if you have been in one organization for a long time. You guess that approaches to selection have probably changed radically since your last interview and this worries you.
- You have been taking a career break to bring up children and feel nervous about re-entering employment.
- Promotion is possible, but to get it you will have to go through an interview, along with other strong candidates.
- You are convinced that you are 'no good' at job interviews and they fill you with dread because you get so nervous.
- You hate the idea of having to *perform* at an interview because you are a modest and unassuming person.

Without the help that a coach can offer, my experience is that outstanding candidates often fail to get the job, innocently sabotaging themselves in ways that have become very familiar to me. This book turns you into your own coach. It's based on twenty years experience of seeing the hiring process from both sides: as an adviser to employers and as a coach preparing people to show the employer what an excellent fit they are for the vacancy.

The book takes the mystery and unhelpful myths out of the job selection process. Reading it and practising the approaches and techniques that I advise will greatly increase your prospects of getting through the interview triumphantly.

Ten top tips for getting the job

Preparation really pays off. If you leave it to the last minute you hugely reduce your chances of getting the job. Here are my ten top tips with more information on each in the chapters that follow:

1. Be certain that as far as possible you really do want the job and know how it will fit your needs and circumstances. Uncertainty looks like lack of commitment to the employer and will mean they rule you out. Why you want the job is one of the most important questions they will ask.

2. Do your research: find out how this job adds value, what the job involves, what's going on for the organization. When you do this – and know how to weave it into your answers – you build your own motivation and also flatter the employer.

3. Employers understand that candidates get jittery but you will benefit from learning some simple techniques for staying calm and centred throughout the process.

4. Plan your interview outfit carefully: it should be an exact match in style and look to whatever the interviewers are likely to wear.

5. An assessment centre is a much fairer way of choosing people than the traditional interview. If you are invited to go through one, feel pleased and relieved. It gives you a much better chance to show what you can do than relying on the interview alone.

6. Enrol a friend or family member to give you a practice interview and to offer you feedback.

7. Most interview questions are completely predictable and you can plan and prepare for them. Offering evidence of how your experience fits the job through skilled storytelling hugely increases your chances of getting it.

4

8. The interview is a social occasion not an exam or an interrogation: treat it as the two-way event it is. You are choosing the selectors as much as they are choosing you. Be enthusiastic, smile.

9. Never negotiate salary and benefits during the interview. After they have said they want you, expect to negotiate on up to three aspects of the offer.

10. Plan your entry into the new role carefully. Take your time to learn what the job really is before plunging into doing it.

DO YOU REALLY WANT THE JOB?

> **❝ Myth**: it's useful to go on 'fishing expeditions' for jobs. It gives you practice at being interviewed
>
> **Reality**: it's better to focus on the job you really want **❞**

Of course you want the job – why else would you put yourself through the torment of being interviewed? But the grip of the 'fishing expedition' idea is powerful: that is, just applying for any old job and hoping that you land an interview, without having any special wish to do the job. Here's why this is not a good idea:

- The more jobs you have on your list, the less you will feel motivated or have time to research the organization and the job – and research is one of the factors that will give you the edge (see chapter 2).
- Possibly the most important single question in the selection process is 'Why do you want this job?' though naïve job-seekers often believe it to be the least important. When you cannot give a convincing answer to this question, or even worse, blurt out that you are unsure, please accept that your chances of getting it are small. Why would an employer want to hire you if you cannot demonstrate your enthusiasm for joining them?
- Variant: Some job-seekers also believe that it's the employer's job to persuade them to accept the job. They simper coyly, thinking that this makes them more desirable. In practice, employers know that over-persuading a reluctant candidate usually leads to a swift exit a few months later with all the consequent costs involved.

So this chapter is a double-check on your motivation. The clearer you are about why the job is a genuinely good fit for you, the more you raise your chances of getting it.

Ideally the push and pull factors need to be in equilibrium. Your reasons for leaving your current employment (the push factors)

9

need to be in perfect balance with your wish for a change (the pull factors). Desperation to leave can cloud your judgement, as can an over-idealized view of what a possible new job will do for you.

The push factors: is it time to move on?

When it is time to make a move, you may have an uneasy feeling that your current job has lost its charm; somehow it does not fulfil some important need. You may have been squashing down your dissatisfaction, but suddenly this is no longer possible. I notice with my own clients that there is often some incident, trivial in itself, which feels as if it sums up everything that is wrong with the job.

> This organization had a Values List. Ha! Ha! It was supposed to define how we worked. Trouble was, no-one took any notice of it. We were supposed, for instance, to put patients first, but in practice what I observed was that senior managers and senior doctors put themselves first. One weekend I was on duty and I had seven patients who could have been discharged and the emergency cover was so thin. In the end this hypocrisy really got to me and I started looking around for another job.

Where disapproval is focused on your boss, this is a particularly bad sign. When you have serious reasons not to respect your boss the whole employment relationship is soured. It is often said that people join organizations but leave managers.

Assessing your current job

Tick the description that seems nearest to your present feelings.

✔

1 Love my job
I spring out of bed every day. The people are great, the culture encourages personal growth; my boss gives me all the support I need. My work has meaning and lines up closely with my personal values.

2 It's pretty good
Most of the time I am motivated. I like and respect my colleagues, I respect what the organization does and I get paid a reasonable amount for the effort I put in. Work energizes me. There are a few little niggles which get on my nerves, but nothing important.

3 It's OK
No such thing as an ideal job – every job has its drawbacks and sometimes these get me down. I plod along fine and I seem to be doing OK, though never quite sure if what I do is recognized or not. Have my doubts about the way the organization is going.

4 Work to live not live to work
It's just a job. It's boring but I have to get on with it because I'm not sure what else I could do. My brain is not engaged most of the time and I slog through the day watching the clock. My real life and interests are outside work – that's where I get the buzz. I feel underpaid and undervalued.

5 It's toxic
I hate my job. Often feel like diving under the duvet on a Monday. If I've got a cold I don't go in. Most of the time I wish I was somewhere else. This organization is killing itself with the way it treats people. No one gives you any feedback or help, then you get blamed when things go wrong.

If you have ticked 1 or 2 it is unlikely that you are serious about making a move. Assuming you have ticked 3, 4 or 5, in an ideal world, what would make you more satisfied?

Factor	Ideally, what would you see, hear, experience?	How far you have this now on a 1–10 scale
Colleagues		
What would be rewarded		
How you'd be rewarded		
Degree of freedom		
Boss		
Nature of your work		
Skills you'd be using		
Challenges you'd face		
Team environment		
Physical environment		
Hours		
Why the work/ job would matter		

Finally

Log the plusses and minuses of your current role.

On the plus side	On the minus side
•	•
•	•
•	•
•	•
•	•

Some questions

How much weight do you give to any of the above factors? Star the ones that matter to you most.

How likely is it that any current dissatisfaction is just a short-term blip?

If you do nothing, what will happen?

How far could your current job be improved – for instance through promotion, training, or just as a result of a conversation with your boss?

How motivated are you to make a change?

	✔
Highly: want to get going right now!	
Reasonably: can't keep postponing	
So-so: a bit worried but OK	
Frightened: but might be up for it	
Can't think about it now	

The pull factors

Two things are generally going on here. One is the thread of motivation that will be consistent throughout your life. The other is the

13

way you will build on this motivation through your interests and skills – and this will vary with time and context. I invite you to complete all three of the following exercises, each designed to give you a different lens on the answer to the questions of what really motivates you and what needs you must satisfy to be happy in a new job.

Being 'in flow'

When you are 'in flow' time passes seamlessly, you are conscious of using all your skills smoothly, there is real joy and no self-doubt, whatever task you are working on seems stretching but achievable and there is some tangible reward. When you look back at this event or period in your life, you feel pride and pleasure.

- Take a large piece of paper. Have a pen and a highlighter ready.
- Now think about three or four times in your career when you were at your best and experienced being 'in flow'. This could be the whole of one period of employment, a particular project or even just one day. What actually happened? Who else was there? What did you learn about yourself? What made each event or time so enjoyable?
- Write down all the key words that occur to you as you remember these moments.
- Now use a highlighter to pick out the most important elements for you.
- Review your list of words: what jumps out for you about what you must have to feel happy and fulfilled at work? Make a list of these elements.

Identifying your personal drivers

All of us have drivers in our lives – needs that motivate us. They are underpinned by deeply held values and beliefs. This activity will help you uncover what your drivers and values are. There are no rights and wrongs. Put a cross to indicate the strength of each

14

driver for you. 10 represents a really strong driver for you, 1 an area where you have little interest. When you have finished, join the points up to make a zig zag. This makes it easier to read and interpret.

PERSONAL DRIVERS, VALUES AND BELIEFS	1	2	3	4	5	6	7	8	9	10
Recognition: getting recognized for achievement; being energized by feedback and attention; enjoying the limelight; performing	–	–	–	–	–	–	–	–	–	–
Influence, competing, having authority, being competent, constantly improving performance in self and others; being an expert in your field	–	–	–	–	–	–	–	–	–	–
Amusement and fun; living life to the full; feeling free to spend time as you wish; making leisure and family time your focus	–	–	–	–	–	–	–	–	–	–
Working for good causes; helping less fortunate people; promoting social justice; doing something for your community	–	–	–	–	–	–	–	–	–	–
Loving and being loved; giving and receiving affection; creating deep one-to-one trust and intimacy with others	–	–	–	–	–	–	–	–	–	–
Feeling connected; friendship, enjoying team projects; liking being part of a group	–	–	–	–	–	–	–	–	–	–
Moral interests; interest in spirituality and ethical/moral questions	–	–	–	–	–	–	–	–	–	–
Safety and security; long-term security and predictability of employment and income	–	–	–	–	–	–	–	–	–	–

15

PERSONAL DRIVERS, VALUES AND BELIEFS	1	2	3	4	5	6	7	8	9	10
Being entrepreneurial; pursuing business and financial interests; financial strategy and planning; dealing, buying and selling	–	–	–	–	–	–	–	–	–	–
Artistic work; creativity; self expression; aversion to the ordinary; being independent	–	–	–	–	–	–	–	–	–	–
Managing, leading and organizing; making things happen as a boss, relishing the buzz of organization life										
Scientific interests: scientific research and discovery; puzzles and mysteries; problem solving	–	–	–	–	–	–	–	–	–	–
Other:	–	–	–	–	–	–	–	–	–	–

Now take a pen in a different colour and draw where you are in your current job on this grid. What does this reveal about any gaps that a new job would fill?

When you combine these two exercises, what does it suggest about the answers to these questions?

In what circumstances are you at your best?

What types of people are you most comfortable with?

When are you really 'in flow' – when time seems to fly by and you know you are doing well?

What kind of organizational context is there – e.g. is it one where there are many creative people? where there is an emphasis on order and practical matters? on customer service? or perhaps on problem solving? Or scientific and intellectual activity?

What subjects do you return to again and again?

What values does this exercise reveal for you?

What is the most important core driver/motivator for you?

What types of relationship do you seem to need to support you at work?

How much do you need to work in a team? How much do you prefer to do a lot of your work alone?

How do you get started? Are there any special triggers for you?

What sorts of results motivate you?

Your strengths

One way of looking at strengths is to think of them as skills and talents some of which are inborn and some learned. The learned behaviours are more likely to be draining of energy than the ones that are inborn. When you are at a career cross roads, it is valuable to know which is which. You should be looking for a job where you minimize the draining activities and maximize the ones that are energy-giving.

> *David* earns a living as a freelance management trainer. He feels a vague sense of dissatisfaction with his work even though it is lucrative and he gets much positive feedback while doing it. David slowly realizes that he enjoys the process of refining the ideas on which his courses are based much more than the business of delivering them to a group. His true interest is in theory and he spends a significant amount of money on materials such as books and magazines that will maintain this interest. David successfully refocuses his search for work on university business schools where his interest in theory can be indulged and – in the best sense – exploited.

We may also have talents which are semi-hidden and which need to emerge, as well as straightforward weaknesses – things we should make every effort to avoid. These will be things we have never done well, could most probably never learn to do well and

17

will therefore take agonizingly long to do to a poor standard and are most definitely draining. To find what this latter category is for you, consider what kinds of tasks always lead you to procrastinate.

Use the diagram below to identify what these categories are for you.

You can also take the *Realise2* questionnaire from the Centre for Applied Positive Psychology where for a small cost you will get a unique report based on these quadrants.

Unrealized strengths To be developed e.g. through training, secondments	***Realized strengths*** ***Known strengths: energy-giving*** Maximize their use
Weaknesses: skills, tasks that take a long time to do to a poor standard To be avoided at all cost	***Learned behaviours: energy-draining*** Minimize their use

The golden quadrant in this grid[†] is on the top right. The questions here as you contemplate any new job are

● How far will this job offer me the chance to get even more value and enjoyment from my strengths?
● How likely is it that this organization will encourage the growth of these strengths?

† Adapted with kind permission from CAPP The Strengths Book: Be Confident, Be Successful, and Enjoy Better Relationships by Realising the Best of You, by Alex Linley, Janet Willars and Robert Biswas-Diener. Published by CAPP Press, 2010, www.cappeu.com

The relevant website is www.strengths2020.com

18

- How much of the job would involve calling on my learned strengths, and therefore be potentially draining?
- How much of this possible new job would require me to work in my weak areas? If so, how much support would there be?

Clare is a recent graduate hoping to move into a career in the voluntary sector. She is a bold, lively personality and can plan and organize well and has been given positive feedback on this in all the temporary jobs she has done since leaving university. But her real enjoyment – and the activities that give her energy – come from using her gifts with disabled children, especially in the outdoors where her talent as a horsewoman can also be put to good use. Clare's jobsearch will focus on roles that allow her to maximize the energy-giving strengths of working directly with children, using her talent with horses. She will seek to downplay the organizing side – a set of skilis she has learnt but that she finds draining. She is also drawn to teaching but has had no training here and ideally wants a job which will give her formal opportunities to develop what she believes is an innate skill. Clare's weaknesses all involve working with routine detail, especially financial detail, and she is determined to avoid any job that asks for this.

Salary

Most people hope to improve their salary when they change jobs, but sometimes the improvement may be small or the job may actually offer less than you were previously earning. This may mean that you will have to think hard about the salary you assume you must deserve.

Michael had been rewarded with a generous salary which had risen steeply in his last few years in the job. Unfortunately it was clear that he and his new boss did not get on and, with the business under severe financial pressure, Michael lost his job. Michael's sector was shrinking and he saw literally no jobs at the same level for which he could apply during six months of diligent job search. His conclusion was that he had been seriously over-paid in his previous role and needed to review his expectations about salary.

In thinking about this, pride and emotion can get in the way. It's all too easy to get fixated on a figure which symbolically represents your value, forgetting that tax will significantly reduce the difference between this notional figure and what you are offered as salary in terms of what you actually take home. And it may sometimes be more important to have a job, any job, than to be unemployed or struggle along with a languishing freelance career.

Decision making starts with working out what your essential expenses are. Use this table to work out what you currently spend and to consider whether and how some might be discretionary or at least reduced.

Monthly expenses

Housing	£	Potential for reduction?
Mortgage or rent		
Council tax		
Insurance		
Service charges		
Maintenance: including cleaning		
Utilities: gas, electricity, water		
Total		

Entertainment/media/holidays	£	Potential for reduction?
TV: licence and subscriptions		
Internet/broadband		
Phone		
Cinema, theatre, DVDs		
Holidays		
Eating out		
Total		

Miscellaneous	£	Potential for reduction?
Clothing		
Food and cleaning materials		
Car		
Grooming: e.g. hair, cosmetics		

continued

Miscellaneous	£	Potential for reduction?
Loan repayments		
Regular savings – e.g. pension		
Child/elder care		
Medical, dental		
Fitness: gym, sporting clubs		
Travel to work		
Pet expenses		
Gifts/donations		
Total		
Overall total		

I realized that I did not need a three bedroom house and could trade down if necessary. I did not need designer clothing or ready meals from supermarkets, or a gym subscription when I could walk everywhere instead. I could entertain friends at home. I did not need mega-bucks holidays – in fact I prefer simple and cheap. Living in London where public transport is so brilliant, a car was just a vanity possession. On the other hand, my cinema visits were an essential part of life's enjoyment and there was no way I could give up my cat, even though every visit to the vet seems to cost a fortune. When I did this sum, I understood that I did not have to find a job with a huge salary like the one I had before. In fact I could work for half that amount and still have plenty left over. This was very liberating indeed and focused me on finding a job that was truly satisfying and not just a money-making machine.

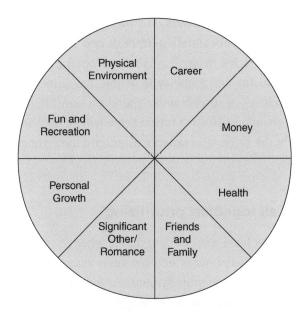

Directions: The eight sections in the Wheel of Life represent balance. Regarding the centre of the wheel as 0 and the outer edge as 10, rank your level of satisfaction with each life area by drawing a straight or curved line to create a new outer edge. The new perimeter of the circle represent the Wheel of Life. How bumpy would the ride be if this were a real wheel?

Where does a job fit with the rest of your life?

No one ever makes a career decision in a vacuum. Work is just one part of life, albeit an important one for many of us. Frequently there are other factors which have to be taken into account. As a final exercise on what you want from any new job, fill in this pie chart. It's a well-known coaching exercise which asks you to rate your satisfaction with your life on a 1–10 scale.

What impact will the other seven wedges need to have on your choice of new job? For instance, if your health is poor, then you may need a job which minimizes travel or physical effort. If you have school-age children, you may be reluctant to move out of a particular catchment area. If your balance of work to fun and leisure is seriously compromised currently then you may want to reconsider whether or not to apply for a job which you know is likely to make similar demands on your time and energy. Be realistic. Few jobs are an absolutely perfect fit and some compromise is usually necessary. For instance, if you are looking for a promotion in the same sector and same type of job and same geographical area your chances of success will depend on how big that sector is and therefore on how likely it is that there will be another employer with exactly the right job available at exactly the right time to suit you.

Putting it all together: prioritizing

You should now have a lot of data about what you want and need from a job and also about which personal values you need to see honoured in any future employment. As a final exercise, use this grid to prioritize what you are looking for.

Step 1

Fill in the shaded column first – just write down items in any order by reviewing all the ideas you have about what you are looking for in a new job. Ideally you should have ten, but the technique will work for more or fewer. Examples might be 'the chance to travel'; 'the opportunity to organize my own work'; 'direct contact with x or y kind of person', 'minimum salary of £x' and so on.

Step 2

In the grids on the right, compare item 1 with item 2, circling whichever is most important to you, then continue down the grid, comparing item 1 with item 3, item 2 with item 3 and so on until you have got to the end of the grid.

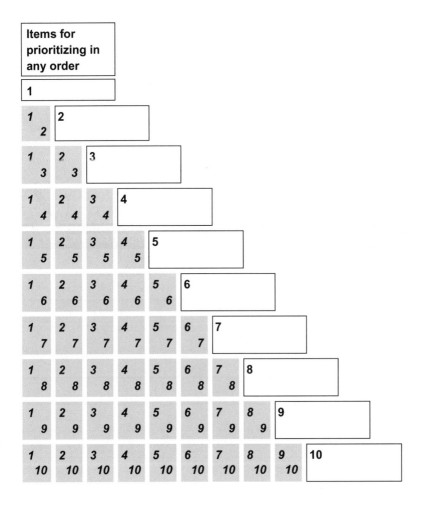

Items for prioritizing in any order
1

| 1 | 2 |
| 2 | |

| 1 | 2 | 3 |
| 3 | 3 | |

| 1 | 2 | 3 | 4 |
| 4 | 4 | 4 | |

| 1 | 2 | 3 | 4 | 5 |
| 5 | 5 | 5 | 5 | |

| 1 | 2 | 3 | 4 | 5 | 6 |
| 6 | 6 | 6 | 6 | 6 | |

| 1 | 2 | 3 | 4 | 5 | 6 | 7 |
| 7 | 7 | 7 | 7 | 7 | 7 | |

| 1 | 2 | 3 | 4 | 5 | 6 | 7 | 8 |
| 8 | 8 | 8 | 8 | 8 | 8 | 8 | |

| 1 | 2 | 3 | 4 | 5 | 6 | 7 | 8 | 9 |
| 9 | 9 | 9 | 9 | 9 | 9 | 9 | 9 | |

| 1 | 2 | 3 | 4 | 5 | 6 | 7 | 8 | 9 | 10 |
| 10 | 10 | 10 | 10 | 10 | 10 | 10 | 10 | 10 | |

Step 3

Fill in the table below, looking back on your grid to see how many times you ringed each item. On the final line, write the order in which you have ranked each item.

1	2	3	4	5	6	7	8	9	10	Item number
										How many times did you ring that item?
										Final ranking

25

Step 4

Now write out your list of priorities in the final order. This should give you some robust guidance on what you want and need in any job for which you have been shortlisted. You may also like to compare how well your present job stacks up against this list of priorities.

Priorities	Comparison with prospective job?
1	
2	
3	
4	
5	
6	
7	
8	
9	
10	

Step 5

Is it worth progressing to the interview?

In summary

Your chances of getting a job are greatly increased if you are strongly motivated. Motivation comes from knowing that the job itself meets important inner needs for you, plays to your strengths and is a strong match with your personal values and drivers. At the same time, it needs to fit well with everything else that is going on in your life. You will be a parent to your children and a son or daughter to your parents, a friend to your friends and – we hope – a partner to your partner – long after you have left even the most exciting job behind. When all of this is in perfect alignment you will be well placed to do yourself justice at the job interview.

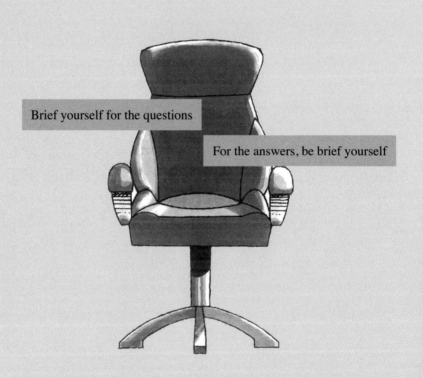

Brief yourself for the questions

For the answers, be brief yourself

2 DOING YOUR RESEARCH

> **❝ Myth**: there's no point in putting too much effort into preparation because you may not get the job
>
> **Reality**: The person who does the most research is the one with the best chance **❞**

Common mistakes

Many candidates for jobs vastly undervalue the importance of this phase. Some people will also say that it's not 'worth' doing any research because they are still not sure whether they want the job. This is peculiarly self-defeating. Research is the way to check out your doubts. If research justifies the doubts, then you can withdraw. I have also had clients tell me that it's 'better' to come to the interview with their minds 'uncluttered by knowing too much about the organization'. As a consultant advising organizations I have more than once seen candidates who began the interview by asking, 'What is it that your department/ organization actually does?' In one such case, the hiring manager snapped back, 'If you don't know that, then let's end this conversation right now'. That interview lasted all of four minutes. Another candidate answered the 'why do you want the job?' question by gushing that she was thrilled with the idea of working in retail. The trouble was that it was a wholesale, not a retail business. This kind of candidate may also declare that they are 'too busy' to do the research. Too busy with what, I wonder? If you want a new job, it becomes your job to do the preparation.

Other candidates do indeed dedicate themselves to research but it is the wrong kind of research. For instance, they will spend hours on the internet mugging up on legislation, reading books and articles on technical aspects of the role or studying policy documents. Most of this is a waste of time: difficult to take in, impossible to prioritize and often of no direct relevance to the job itself.

Why research is essential

No employer is a charity – even when they are technically a charity. All jobs cost the employer money and the only thing any employer is interested in is whether you will deliver value. They are not really interested in you, your needs, your private life, your quirky little hobbies and past history. They are only interested in what you will bring. This means that the cost of employing you must be outweighed by the benefit you will create. Unless you are self-employed, you may be innocent about this. For instance, you may assume that the job just costs the employer your actual salary. In practice you should at least double and possibly triple your salary to find the real cost. The real cost includes recruitment, premises, tax, admin support, managerial time, the marketing and training budgets . . . the list is endless.

How jobs add value

The only reason that any job exists is to create value. You create value by reducing cost and increasing turnover. This applies regardless of whether the organization is in the profit or non-profit sector. Here are some examples:

An in-house health and safety trainer teaches people how to avoid the accidents and compensation claims that could otherwise cost the company literally millions.

A waiter handles customers with such charm and well-placed enthusiasm about the menu that people return and also recommend the restaurant to other customers.

An estates management expert keeps the infrastructure of the building running, thus preventing expensive downtime. One maintenance engineer was able to demonstrate in his job interview that he could save the company around a million dollars through more efficient use of the heating system.

If a job does not add value it will eventually be eliminated or something cheaper will be devised. Where the employer believes in the economic necessity of the job but not the person currently doing it, the person doing it will be fired while the job survives. An employer is not interested in you unless you can demonstrate that you would repay their investment in you by adding value. To be able to make such a claim, you need to do the research.

Employer vanity

All employers want to believe that you have personally selected them. Even where a business is clearly failing, the employer will wish to believe in your dedication to their cause. All employers believe that it is a privilege to join their staff. They loathe the idea that as a candidate you see their job vacancy as *just a job*. It makes them feel that you arc using them. The more research you do, and the more you demonstrate that you have done it, the more likely they are to believe in your enthusiasm.

In doing the research you should focus on these areas:

Financial results

How do this year's results compare with the last three or four?

Are they forecasting a profit for the coming year?

What do the most senior people in the organization earn?

If they are a listed company, what has happened to their share price over the last few years?

Strategic trends

What overall trends are there in this organization's world? How could these trends benefit or damage it?

Customers/clients

Who are their customers? What purchases are they typically making? What are they seeking when they make a purchase? This is often not a physical entity but an experience: excitement, enlightenment, entertainment.

Competitors

Who are their competitors? How well are they doing? Who might be taking a slice out of their market?

Regulators

How do their regulators see them? How well are they performing against ethical or other targets?

The job itself

Where does this job fit in the organization? How is it meant to add value and what value?

Culture

What's it actually like working in this organization? This will always be different from the face it presents to the outside world.

How to do the research

Annual reports: Limited companies post their results and these are easy to access. PLCs also produce annual reports for shareholders. If the report is not available on the internet, you can ask for a copy by saying you are interested in buying shares.

Regulators' reports: Public sector organizations normally post these on their websites. If they have been conspicuously failing, they might also have been the focus of special enquiries with a publicly available report. Marita, a nurse, started her own investigation this way when she was researching a hospital that she was considering joining.

> First of all the report on their website was in tiny type – I could scarcely read it. As I went on through it I saw why. They had not impressed. Their scores on cleanliness were as low as they could possibly be. Their clinical outcomes were well below par too. Funnily enough this did not put me off. I could see where and why there might be a role for me

> as my speciality is infection control and all the research I did on them showed me that they had a real problem here – for instance their rates of MRSA were far higher than they should have been.

If a public sector organization does not have the results of inspections and audits on its own website, you can normally expect to read them on the regulators' own websites.

Staff surveys: useful for getting an impression of the culture; how people feel about working there. Most large organizations now carry out an annual survey of staff satisfaction. If this is not available on the organization's website, you may be able to ask someone inside the company to email it to you.

'Mystery shopping': useful for seeing the organization as its customers and clients see it. Mystery shopping is one of the most powerful market research techniques. People posing as purchasers investigate the customer experience. Marita, the nurse quoted above did this.

> I went into the hospital four times, posing as a visitor looking for a non-existent patient on about ten wards. Although there was an anti-bacterial gel dispenser at the entrance to every ward, and another in every bay, I saw literally no one use them. One of the main ways that infection is spread in hospitals is through visitors, not staff. I also noticed that the main corridor from one part of the hospital to another consistently had a rime of dirt and dust along the skirtings. It didn't look as if it was cleaned properly or very often.

You can do the same: try calling the main switchboard and asking for some kind of help; visit the premises and see how you are dealt with at reception; if the organization is in retail, buy and then return some goods and assess how efficiently and helpfully you are treated. Look at what is on the walls and how tidy or not the premises are. Look at whether the staff seem cheerful.

35

Website: useful as an all purpose source of information. The website tells you a great deal about how an organization sees itself and also about how it wants the world to see it. Questions to ask yourself:

Is the site easy to navigate?

What visual impression does it give you of the organization's true identity?

Is its information useful?

How does the tone strike you? Friendly? Impersonal?

How well is it written – e.g. free from factual, spelling and punctuations errors?

If it invites you to make contact – and you do – how quickly do you get a response?

Trade or sector magazines: There is bound to be a specialist magazine or website devoted to the sector and your target organization will probably have appeared in it at some point. Once you have identified the magazine you will probably have to log on as a subscriber – normally this will be free – to explore how the organization appears in its sector.

Informal personal contacts: useful for individual views on the job and the organization. Who do you know in the organization? Who do you know who knows someone in the organization? Contact these people and explain your mission: to understand what goes on in the organization, what its strengths are, what problems it faces.

If you can contact the person whose resignation or retirement has created the vacancy, do so, but take their responses with a degree of scepticism. They have left for some good reason and you may receive a cynical or one-sided response. People employed in the organization will always give you many clues, some inadvertent, about what it is like working there. For instance, if there is a high moan-level, ask yourself what has led to this victim mentality. Good questions to ask here are:

How does this job add value for the organization?

What problems does it solve?

What are the outstanding problems that are waiting to be solved by the new person?

What do you need to do to succeed in this organization?

What would your advice be about how to do this particular job well?

Specialist websites: These spring up and die down all the time. Most are offering reports for money on the principle that they can save the buyer many hours of research time. Some are free. Most are selective in the companies they include. It may also be worth searching Wikipedia, the Wall St Journal, Fortune or the Financial Times websites. Another tip is to enter 'the truth about <name of your target company>' or '<name of your target company> review' to see what comes up. This often leads to interesting stories and reports, but bear in mind that much of this may be tittle-tattle.

Competitors: All organizations have competitors, even if they are internal competitors or other organizations in the public sector. Send for their brochures or try their services and see how it feels at first hand. It is usually relatively easy to find out who the competitors are and what they offer. This is what Stefan discovered when he was preparing for an internal promotion.

> When I was shortlisted for the job of Team Leader for one part of Legal Services I realized that this department, in which I was already a member of staff, had loads of internal as well as external competitors. What was happening was that various rival lawyers had sprung up in different bits of the organization. They had appointed their own mini legal teams and also a tradition had grown up of buying in legal help from outside, I thought unnecessarily – and of course

37

this was also a cash cost to the organization. I arranged visits to each of the other teams and their bosses just to see what it was that they were providing and why. This was sobering and revealing. The general view of our department was that it was slow, expensive and behind the times. I was shocked to realize we had become complacent and lazy. It totally changed the way I made my pitch for the job and I feel sure that this was why I got it.

Checking out the panel

Ask who will be taking part in the selection process. It is easy to google the boss and any of the rest of the panel. Sometimes this takes you to minutes of meetings attended by the people concerned, sometimes it will take you to personal websites or to social networking sites such as Linkedin or Facebook. Where people have spoken at conferences, you may be able to download their presentations, getting a fast track to their opinions and concerns.

How to use this research: some dangers to avoid

We are a multi-cultural society and many organizations are global concerns. Make sure that you do not commit blunders here. For instance, would you know how to pronounce these names? Would you know whether they are men or women?

Jianguo Liu

Zainabu Al Jumeam

Sasha Sergeyevich Ivanov

VV (Valvettiturai) Prabhakaran

Protocol varies from culture to culture about using people's names. First names are sometimes family names or indicate ethnic and religious origins or even place of birth. So would you for instance know

Whether Mohammed Umah should be addressed as Mr Umah? Could you address him as Mohammed at a first meeting?

With Kim Su Yong is it Mr Kim or Mr Yong – or neither?

There are traps too in names that seem familiar because they have been anglicized. So a Russian Boris is actually pronounced Bah-rees.

Company names

Pay particular attention to how people inside the company refer to it. For instance, no one inside the BBC refers to it as The Beeb or The Corporation. It's The Mitsubishi Corporation, not Mitsubishi. You may find out during your research that people inside the organization refer to it in a particular way, but that does not give you permission to do the same. Inside the British Foreign and Commonwealth Office (FCO) which many years ago used to be The Foreign Office, staff refer to it as The Office. But if you were applying from the outside, you would refer to it as 'The FCO'. To call it 'The Foreign Office' will merely show how out of date you are. Insiders refer to the pharmaceutical company as 'AZ' but you must refer to it as AstraZeneca and note that in writing about it, it is AstraZeneca without a space between the two syllables. In general it is safer to refer to the full name of the organization and not to abbreviate, unless the abbreviation is actually how the organization refers to itself in public – for instance, BBC, M&S.

> I was researching a small advertising company, had an interview lined up and was desperate to join because it was full of young, talented people who did brilliant work and I wanted to be one of them! I arranged to meet two people, both older than me, who worked there, for an after-work drink to pump them for info. Let's call the company Cheek Creatives Ltd. After two glasses of wine, I started copying these two very nice guys and referring to 'CCL' or 'Cheeky'.

One of them gently interrupted me and said, Mike, you haven't joined us yet. When you have, you can say CCL or Cheeky. For now, just refer to it as Cheek Creatives. Gulp! I remember blushing a little but also being just so grateful. It could really have grated if I'd done it at the interview.

Company dress codes

One of the reasons that it is always an excellent idea to visit the organization in person is to check out how people look. Be aware that

Junior people may dress differently from their more senior colleagues

Different departments may have different dress codes

You may be visiting on a 'dress down' day, especially if it is a Friday

There may be subtle differences in formality between what it is permissible for women to wear as opposed to men

Even in organizations where people habitually dress informally, it may be customary to dress formally for job interviews

During your visit make a note, for instance, of whether the men wear ties and what colour and style their shirts are; whether women with long hair are pinning it up or leaving it loose, who, if anyone, is wearing a suit; what kind of jewellery is on show; whether bright colours predominate or whether you see a universal black. One of your questions during your contacts with people working in the organization is to ask directly for advice about interview clothing. There is more about image in chapter 6.

Warning

You have carried out brilliantly thorough research. You believe you could write a PhD thesis on the organization, its strengths, its weaknesses. You almost believe you are already working there. You could sort everything out. Believe me you could not, because you are still looking at it from the outside. So although you absolutely must do this research, there is an art in knowing how to use what you have discovered and I deal with this in chapters 8 and 11.

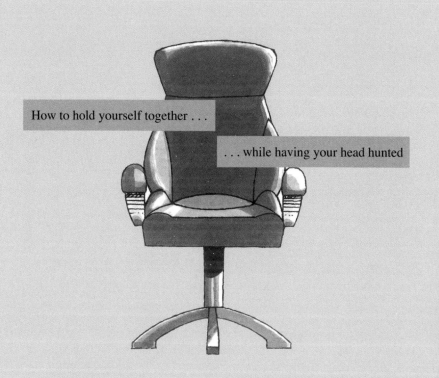

How to hold yourself together . . .

. . . while having your head hunted

3 WORKING WITH PROFESSIONAL RECRUITERS

> **"Myth**: the recruiter's job is to find you a job
> **Reality**: the recruiter is working for the employer and is not really interested in you **"**

Recruitment consultants are only responsible for a small percentage of the jobs market, but when you do encounter one, or wish to, it is important to know how best to manage the process.

First you should understand which bit of this sector you are in.

Job Centres are a state-sponsored initiative offered to employers and candidates alike. They combine policing benefits claims with careers advice – a blend that contains a conflict of interest that can be confusing to both staff and candidate. In effect the Job Centre is a free employment agency that also offers help with CVs, interview techniques and job searches.

Recruitment Agencies operate in specific sectors – for instance, sales, catering, nursing, social work, IT, social care, teaching, office services – usually working out of high street shops and online. They may offer jobs at professional, semi-skilled and unskilled levels, either temporary or permanent. The employer may pay a flat fee for a permanent member of staff or may pay a regular percentage of a temp's salary. Recruitment agencies can add value for employers by offering to test the skills claimed by a candidate. So, for instance, if you are looking for a job as a senior PA, you should expect the agency to test your claim to type at 120 words per minute. Similarly, for jobs needing fluency in a foreign language, some agencies will administer sophisticated assessments. A careful agency will take the trouble to review your skills with you – in effect running a practice interview – and will then groom you for the job by briefing you thoroughly. Where the agency has built a long-standing, successful relationship with the employer, they will be able to pass on to you a great deal about that employer and will only put forward candidates whom they believe to be a good fit for both the job and the organization. Some agencies will also re-write your CV for you.

You can make it easy for recruitment agencies to help you by

- Being candid about your skills and not making over-blown claims
- Preparing a detailed CV so that they can help you tailor it if necessary to a particular employer
- Being specific about the kind of work you are looking for
- Forming a relationship of mutual trust with an individual consultant wherever possible.

However, in general these companies are interested in long-term relationships with employers rather than with candidates. They look for quick turnover and high volume and, although friendly and professional, may in practice have little time to devote to you as a job-seeking individual.

Executive Search Consultants ('head-hunters')

Executive Search Consultants or 'head-hunters' are retained to find senior candidates for highly paid jobs. Their role is not to act as your personal job-search companion. They do not find people jobs, they find people *for* jobs. Head-hunters prefer to approach rising stars already well settled in their current role. They are much less interested if you are unemployed. This is because they like to offer the potential employer the candidates who seem like scarce, highly prized commodities. This is why head-hunters prefer to approach than to be approached.

There is no point in randomly sending out your CV. The average amount of time a recruitment consultant spends on reading an unsolicited CV is about ten seconds before discarding it, or alleging that it will be 'stored on our database' (believe that at your peril).

The standard of professionalism varies wildly from people who are sensitive, skilled and thoroughly scrupulous in everything they do to people who are unskilled and disgracefully idle. Never work with a head-hunter until you have established where they are on this spectrum.

Head-hunters can work on a contingency basis; that is, they are hired for one-off searches and paid if one of their candidates is appointed. This is the most common form of contract between commissioning client and head-hunter. The normal fee is 30% of the successful candidate's first year salary, and payment may be withheld until the appointed candidate has been in place for at least six months and has passed their probationary period. More rarely, head-hunters are retained by an organization over a period of years. Where this is the case, you can normally expect a much more thorough screening process which will include psychometric testing and possibly a little coaching.

Head-hunters are essentially salespeople who first of all sell their services to the employer, and later on sell the vacancy to the strongest candidates. The best of them have extensive knowledge of recruitment practices in the sectors where they work and also have long-standing relationships with senior employers. However, the skills they have in advising and coaching tend to be added later, if at all, so it is sensible not to expect too much here while hoping to be pleasantly surprised.

Scammers and frauds

This is a sector full of scammers, so be warned. If you are approached out of the blue and offered 'job search help' or 'career management services', be very suspicious. The purpose of the call could be any of the following: identity theft, trying to sell you expensive careers advice, offers to sell you 'secret' information about companies which in fact is freely available on the internet, trying to steal a march on other head-hunters.

Screening the screeners

If the person who contacts you is unknown to you, research the company and the individual thoroughly before taking any further steps. Look at the website and google any individuals involved. Ask for references. Ask how long they have been in business and what kinds of candidates and for what roles they have successfully placed people. Have faith in your instincts about how far you trust or like any of the individuals you meet. Not all are likeable or trustworthy. Refuse to give sensitive personal data on the phone, for instance about your date and place of birth, your mother's maiden name or your citizenship status. Where scamming is involved, refusing to give this information means that this is the last you will hear from the caller.

Finding the right search consultant

Ideally you need to have on your side two or three high-powered recruitment consultants from different firms. But this can feel like an exasperatingly circular process. If you don't know any head-hunters, how do you find them? And if their basic way of operating is don't call us, we'll call you, how do you attract their attention in the first place?

Successful head-hunters know that any of their contacts could be useful in three ways: as commissioning clients, as referrers and as candidates. The best of them will therefore aim to keep in touch with a star performer over a period of years, knowing that someone who starts as a candidate could turn into a commissioner and will also be useful as a contact. The entire head-hunting operation is about personal networking. Who are the influential people in the sector? Who is on the way up? Who could be ready for a move if the right tempting offer were made? Who knows someone who knows someone who could indiscreetly tell a so-called secret concerning what the true story is about this or that organization? Some head-hunters enjoy their reputation for dark arts where job-finding is concerned. For others, being involved in finding the right person at a senior level for a household-name company is understandably exciting and gives a pleasing feeling of being at the centre of things. Some of the best head-hunters are in it for the thrill of the chase, which is why their nickname is well-earned.

All of these methods could work in finding a head-hunter:

- When you are approached as a 'referrer', that is as someone who might be able to suggest a possible candidate, first ask what sectors and types of organization they work for. Be friendly and helpful and offer any names you think might be of interest. Check the head-hunter's company website, google the individual, note the name and keep it for reference. If it sounds as if they might recruit for the kind of job you are seeking, let them know that in principle you could also be in the market for a move. Don't sound desperate and don't go into detail. Ask whether it would be worth sending your CV. If the answer is lukewarm, then it is probably not worth pressing the point. If you get an enthusiastic response, send the CV and follow it up with a phone call suggesting a meeting.

- Where you have been approached or have been a candidate in the past, keep the relationship going. Head-hunters frequently change firms, in fact they are often head-hunted themselves, but this does not matter since it is the personal contact that is important.

- Where you have a friend or colleague who has been in touch with or been placed by a head-hunter, ask for the name. Call the head-hunter mentioning your colleague's name and proceed as above.

- Where you know you are going to be made redundant, consult the most senior HR professional in your current organization for head-hunter suggestions. Don't do this unless it is known that you will be leaving. HR works for the organization not for you and whatever promises are made about confidentiality, it would be unwise to trust to this.

- Quality newspapers have appointments sections where head-hunters and their clients hedge their bets with advertisements. Where the head-hunter's name is given and it appears that they are operating in your sector and at your level, but that particular job is clearly not for you, call the individual and give them a brief version of your current situation, a swift summary of your skills and what you are looking for. Offer to send your CV.

49

- Consult a directory. One of the market leaders here is *Executive Grapevine* which gives detailed information on search companies. You may be able to find it in larger libraries or your HR department may subscribe. Look for people who are operating in your sector and then approach them as above.
- Where the salary and your ideal job is on the margins of what high-street recruitment agencies and head-hunters might deal with, consider approaching high-street agencies which have specialized professional departments.

Once a meeting has been arranged, you should pay attention to how you are treated and how you feel while on their premises.

> The offices were very glossy and there was a heavily made up receptionist in a bright red suit that looked like some sort of corporate uniform. I thought she looked more like someone on a beauty counter than a professional person and I also thought, 'Who's paying for all this glitz?' It was meant to impress, but I didn't like it.

> The consultant agreed to see me as a favour to a friend but he took no trouble to disguise his many yawns during our conversation. Maybe he'd had a heavy day or something but what it conveyed to me was that he found me and/or his job very boring. I wasn't surprised when he finally announced that he didn't think he would be able to find anything for me but I couldn't have worked with someone that rude anyway.

Working with head-hunters and other recruiters

When a head-hunter calls you at work, you may be in an open plan office. The head-hunter should ask you whether now is a good time to talk. If you do not have privacy, suggest they call you at home. It is unlikely that the consultant will tell you the actual name of their

50

client company at this point, but you can probe for general information such as, 'How long has this company been in business?' 'Where would this job be based?' 'What kind of salary is on offer?' 'What's the reason for the vacancy?'

Let's suppose that this goes well. So now you have a date with a head-hunter. Don't be fooled by the apparent informality of the approach. You should treat the whole thing exactly like an interview, which is what it is. Remember the consultant is only interested in you if you seem to have exactly what their client is looking for. Speed and efficiency are qualities that impress a head-hunter. They act fast themselves and appreciate it in others. Return calls and emails swiftly. When you say you will call back, do so within the time period you have promised. Don't pester: if your calls and emails are not returned, assume that the consultant has lost interest in you. The usual reason is that your fit with the job is less than the 90% that head-hunters look for. Unless you are a truly red-hot candidate, you will have to make the running in the relationship. Head-hunters are busy and preoccupied. They prioritize their attention for clients not candidates.

Mistakes you should never make include

- Being less than straightforward about your reasons for wanting a change of job – if you do.
- Pretending you don't want a change when you do.
- Referring to him or her as a *head-hunter*, even if everyone else does. Some of them do not like the label. Say 'Search Consultant' instead.
- Divulging salary information too soon. If the head-hunter is vague at the initial phone call stage, and many are, say something like, 'It's difficult to talk about this unless you can give me some idea of the salary range the employer is offering'. If the answer is a sum wildly above or below your current salary then you should say that the job is not a good fit with what you are looking for, unless there are some special compensating circumstances.
- Over- or understating what you want as compensation. So for instance, if you are currently earning £xk and the job on offer

pays £xk × 2 it is unlikely that you will be taken seriously as a candidate. Current salary is always checked as part of the final referee process so be truthful if you do divulge your salary.

- Being indiscreet about your current role and company. No blabbing or blurting: if you would hesitate to say it to the hiring manager then don't say it to the recruiter.
- Approaching more than one consultant in the same firm.
- Dressing sloppily: the consultant's role at this stage is pre-screening so if you do not look the part you will get no further (see chapter 5).
- Failing to give crisp, convincing, confident answers to the recruiter's questions. These are essentially precursors to the questions the employer will also ask so all the principles of how to answer interview questions apply here (see chapters 11 and 12).
- Failing to ask for a cast iron guarantee of confidentiality and discussing protocols around the recruiter approaching a company before they have asked for your permission. The same applies to referees. Some head-hunters will ask for referees' names early in the process. In general it is safer to withhold referee names until the interview stage and even then with caution and only when you have the express permission of the referee.

You should anticipate all the obvious questions and have given thought to the answers. Typical questions head-hunters ask at this stage:

What do you like and dislike about what you are currently doing?

What makes you ready to leave your current job – if you are?

What are the major highlights and low points of your career to date?

What kind of company are you looking to join?

What would be the ideal job for you?

What are your family circumstances? How far have you discussed a change of job with them? Are you willing to re-locate?

What do you currently earn? What kind of compensation are you looking for in a new job?

If this conversation does not progress to the next stage, which ideally is that you are placed on the shortlist for an interview, it is good practice for the head-hunter to offer you feedback on the reasons. Do not expect any great revelations here. The most common feedback is that your experience is not an already perfect fit with what the hiring company is looking for. Don't argue, take it personally or get defensive. You need to keep this head-hunter on your side as he or she took the trouble to consider you and meet you face to face. This suggests that you were at least in the outer ring of suitable candidates. Head-hunters regard time as their most precious asset so if they have made the time to see you they have at least shown some interest in you. Thank the consultant politely and ask for some brief advice about what to do to make your application stronger another time. Say you will keep in touch.

Some candidates feel so aggrieved at this point that they conclude the head-hunter is an idiot whose stupidity is blocking them. They then try to approach the hiring company direct. Never do this: you will annoy both the head-hunter and the company. The company is paying the head-hunter a great deal of money for their judgement and experience and to avoid precisely this kind of confrontation.

The best head-hunters can be brilliantly helpful throughout the whole process. Some have also now trained as coaches and can offer the right blend of support and challenge. The signs of excellence here are that the head-hunter is prepared to devote time to coaching you on your CV and preparing you for the interview. After the interview, regardless of whether you get the job, you should have a full de-brief with frank, skilfully given feedback. When you are the successful candidate the head-hunter will also help you negotiate the best possible deal. You may have this discussion once or twice in a career. Head-hunters are doing it all the time so you should let them take the lead here: they know how to have the conversation. It is in their interests to aim high because this way they benefit too. Once you are actually in the job, the head-hunter should call you to find out how it's going. They will be looking to you for referrals as well as for feedback on whether you and the hiring employer made the right decision.

The best head-hunter relationships are long-term. Keep in regular touch, offering updated CVs from time to time and letting the consultant know, discreetly, when you might be in the market for another move. A mutually beneficial relationship is the one where each party treats the other with friendliness and respect: that is the ideal. Don't expect generalized careers advice from recruitment consultants – that is not their role and most do not have the experience, time or skill to do it. If that is what you want you need a specialist career coach – a different profession. What head-hunters are good at is focused help around particular vacancies, and if you are the right candidate their contribution can make all the difference to your chances of getting the job.

4 MANAGING NERVOUSNESS

> **Myth**: nervousness during the selection process is inevitable; you can't do anything about it and it can prevent you getting the job
>
> **Reality**: some nervousness is helpful and in any case you can learn to control it

My client Mike will stand for many hundreds of others over the years. Mike had come to me because he believed that 'chronic nerves' at the interview stage were going to prevent him finding a new job. Despite the plain evidence that he had been in employment for many years including four previously successful job interviews, his firm belief was that he had got these jobs despite his 'nerves', and that he was hopelessly scuppered by them: 'My hands shake, I stutter, I blush, I sweat . . . it's awful. My brain seizes up and I can't answer the simplest question'. Because of this self-limiting belief, Mike was reluctant to apply for new jobs and as a result had probably missed out on many opportunities to further his career.

Like many such clients, although he truly did believe that he was merely describing a self-evident truth, Mike was grossly exaggerating. He had magnified some small stumbles in interviews, something virtually everyone does, into unbearable humiliations. Mike believed himself to be unique. He talked about having to summon up courage even to 'confess' to me, and described feeling intense shame that as a fully grown man he could be in the grip of something so primitive. Actually, as I told him, a good quarter of the clients I see for job interview coaching have identical worries, so there is nothing unusual in their feelings.

Why is this? The most obvious reason is that when we leave childhood behind, most of us want to create the image of being a competent person. It is rare to be formally rated. Although most organizations now have appraisal systems, there is much research to show how often this is a meaningless exercise in box-ticking with both managers and their staff avoiding any tough discussions of performance. We may take a driving test, or perhaps an occasional exam for a professional qualification, but that's about it. So a job interview can put our claims to be admirable, successful and competent on the line. It's a competition and we may not win. There is other research showing that when asked to rate how we compare with others, most of us claim to be in the top 20% – something that is statistically impossible. So that carefully cultivated self-image may collide with the judgement of others. The questions we ask are things like: 'Will I make a complete fool of myself?' 'Will I be shown up?' 'What if I don't get it, how do I explain myself to people who know I'm applying?'

Nervousness is usually about feeling a lack of control and being unable to deal with the uncertainty that follows. Once the preoccupation with nervousness takes hold, some people then focus their worry on worrying about the nervousness. So, for instance, I have had women clients tell me that they always wear high-neck jumpers for a job interview, even in hot weather, as a way of concealing a flushed neck and chest. This is regardless of whether such a garment is comfortable or flattering; hiding the physical signs of nervousness from the interviewers seems more important. Others confess to dosing themselves with alcohol or drugs, despite being fully aware of the risk that these tactics will create far more problems than they solve.

Worriers typically avoid tackling the issues that are worrying them, dithering endlessly. But avoiding what you are afraid of just reinforces your belief that you could not cope if the worry turned out to be true. Chronic worriers also believe that worrying about the interview is in itself a helpful activity. The truth is that it is not.

You also need to distinguish between what you can control in this process and what you cannot. Pointless worrying about job interviews usually focuses on unanswerable questions such as 'If only I knew they would definitely appoint me I could relax'. This kind of worry generates a further chain of unrolling fantasies all of which end in disaster: 'If I perform badly at this interview, then people will know I'm a fraud, then I'll lose my current job, then I'll lose my social status, then I'll be friendless then my life will be over . . .'

It all starts with what is in your head. Ask yourself how you think about the interview process and what language you use to describe it. Here are some common phrases:

It's like being in a *torture chamber*

I know they'll *interrogate* me

Guantanamo has nothing on it, they'll pin me down and make me *confess* to crimes I didn't commit!

I feel as if I'm *on trial*

I'm *on the rack* the whole time I'm in there

It reminds me of doing an *exam* – just like I felt when I had to do an oral exam for French

If any of this is the mental image you have of a job interview, your first task is to accept how wildly misplaced it is. A job interview is not like being in a courtroom, a torture chamber, a prison or exam hall. All these are metaphors of helplessness and victimhood and you are not helpless or a victim. You have freely chosen to compete for the job and can decide at any point to withdraw.

The interview as a two way process

A much healthier way of thinking about a job interview is that it is a two way process. You are choosing the organization as much as they are choosing you and every wise selector knows this to be the case. In fact the better the fit between you and the job, the more the true power is in the hands of the candidate. When advising organizations on selection, I have seen many times that the panel can become desperate to impress an outstanding candidate, wanting to make the job offer the moment the interview is over.

Putting fears into perspective

Try walking across your room right now. Imagine that you are looking at yourself sitting in your chair. Imagine you are at your most resourceful, wise and sensible. Ask yourself

What advice would the most resourceful version of myself give to me now this minute?

How much will this job interview matter in one/five/ten years' time? (Most probable answer: not at all)

What does this more resourceful version of myself have to tell me about how to manage my worries right now?

> I stood up and looked at 'myself' and thought, 'You idiot. Of course you're well qualified for this job and the truth is that at least three of the other candidates also are. They may well just pick at random because we could all do the job. If you don't get this one you'll get another where the dice will fall your way. And even if you don't you will survive – it's not the end of the world. Work isn't everything. Do your best and – so what?'

Looking at your beliefs

Sometimes my clients will tell me that they believe themselves to be 'suffering from low self-esteem'. There is not a shred of evidence that 'low self-esteem' exists as a crippling psychological condition, secret and shaming, as described in endless self-help books, only what most of the human race experiences much of the time, in other words, some legitimate doubts, occasional guilt and shame and realizing that other people are often better than we are at many of the things we do. What's its opposite? If it is 'high self-esteem', then be afraid. Research shows that people who describe themselves as having high self-esteem tend to be arrogant, have little self-awareness or care for others. High self-esteem is also a characteristic of many criminals and sociopaths.

However, you may have beliefs about yourself that are unhelpful such as

> *I am an impostor, if people knew what I was really like they would shun me*
>
> *I have to be perfect in everything I do*

I must please others – their needs come before mine

I must be competent at all times – failure would be unbearable

I have to be strong – asking for help shows I might be weak

These beliefs have a number of characteristics. In benign form they might be useful – for instance, there might be a grain of truth in them. When you are a worrier, you apply them in a black and white way: they MUST be 100% true. They then have the force of superstition – you feel you must behave as if they are true at all times. Challenge these beliefs by reminding yourself that to be human means making mistakes. There is no human being who is totally perfect. Be realistic about your limitations and also about your strengths.

Distinguishing between useful and pointless worry

A useful worry is based on a problem that is plausible and specific. It is something you can act on right now, as opposed to a pointless worry where there is literally nothing you could do about it immediately. With a useful worry you can move to a specific solution quickly, as opposed to a pointless worry where there is no solution because the problem is too big or too vague. If your concern about a coming job interview is based on a pointless worry, an attempt to answer questions that cannot be answered, or to control what it is not within your gift to control, ask yourself

What can I and should I be doing right now to prepare?
What would make for an answer I could live with?

Catastrophizing

Strange as it may seem, it is also useful to imagine the very worst that can happen, something that chronic worriers notably avoid.

Worry is a refusal to accept reality, not a way of dealing with it. Instead of trying to stop a worrying thought, try naming the worst possibility and repeating it out loud dozens of times. At first anxiety levels go up, but then it becomes routine, and then – boring. Examples:

63

I might lose my way in the presentation – yes, that's possible

I might start one of those awful blushes that start in my legs and roll relentlessly up my body – indeed, it could happen

I might not get this job – true, I might not

They might offer it to me but at a much lower salary that they've advertised – always possible

Having named the most awful thing you can imagine, now ask yourself how you would manage if it happened. I promise you that you would cope – and live with the aftermath. Whatever it is, ask yourself the ultimate shrugging-off question: so what? You would survive. There are worse things that can happen than failing to get a job.

Some strategies that help

'Nerves' are the body's response to fear. Blood pressure and heartbeat go up, skin flushes and sweats. The rush of adrenaline we experience was designed originally to help us fight or run away. This is exactly what we can't do in a job interview, so we have all the symptoms without being able to engage in the physical activity which would help manage the bodily response.

Most panel members expect candidates to be at least a little anxious and will make allowances for a few stumbles and hesitations. Interviewers do not have X-ray vision. They cannot actually see your raised heartbeat or peer into your brain. And it is extremely rare that selectors set out to humiliate or stress you. No sensible employer wants to lose the outstanding person as a result of creating absurdly high levels of anxiety during the selection process and, if they did, would you really want to join an organization that behaved in this way?

Exercise

Vigorous exercise helps discharge the build-up of adrenaline and is thought to create feel-good hormones. Exercise stimulates the brain's pituitary gland into releasing endorphins. These are morphine-like hormones which produce euphoric feelings – a natural 'high'. Even a ten-minute walk can be a help. Obviously you cannot do a full-scale run or jog before an interview if it would mean arriving wonderfully relaxed but also hot and sweaty. But you may be able to walk to the interview venue briskly enough to raise your heartbeat and feel a little warm.

Behaving 'as if'

In the 1951 musical *The King and I*, the main character encourages her young son to 'whistle a happy tune' to disguise his nervousness as she begins her job with the King of Siam. This is good advice. One of the best ways to get over social anxiety is to simulate confidence. Do you really want to seem 'shy' at the interview? Shyness can appear cute – for instance in a child it can look modest, self-effacing and adorable. In a job interview unfortunately it just looks like helplessness or whimsy. So if you are prone to describe yourself as 'shy', stop now. Shyness is just a form of self-absorption and no one wants a self-absorbed employee. Observe and then assume the confident body posture and speech of un-shy people. Behave as if you really are confident. Practise until it becomes second nature and you believe it yourself.

7/11 breathing

This simple technique is reliable and easy to do. It forces your body to slow down and will produce alpha waves in the brain – the calm pattern associated with relaxation. You can do it anywhere and no one will know.

To learn it, set aside 15 minutes where you can guarantee being quiet and uninterrupted. Sit down somewhere comfortable. Make sure both feet are firmly planted on the ground and keep your hands palm down on your lap. Never cross arms or legs when doing this technique as it will create physical tension. Release any rigidity in your shoulders, let them become relaxed and supple. Let the muscles in your face soften. Now start concentrating on your breathing, but don't force it. The aim is to breathe in to a count of 7 and breathe out to a count of 11.

- As you start, just observe how you are tending to breathe. Often what is happening is that the in-breath comes from the upper chest and is longer than the out-breath. This can lead to gulping for air and to hyperventilating where the carbon dioxide element of the blood is reduced, constricts blood vessels, reduces the flow of oxygen and leads to dizziness and more panic. You will be reversing this pattern.
- Focus on breathing in from below your waist and letting your lungs expand to their full extent. When we are tense, this does not happen and is one of the main causes of shortness of breath. Put your hands lightly on to your sides, fingers pointing towards your middle just above the waist. You should feel your hands gently pushed outwards as you breathe in.
- Now start counting the in-breath to 7. At the same rate, let the out-breath lengthen to a count of 11, with no holding or pausing between breathing in and breathing out. Blowing the breath out through an open mouth as if you are steadily blowing out a candle helps release any remaining tension.
- Mentally draw a triangle running from your navel to your hips and imagine it's filled with a balloon which you are inflating and deflating as you breathe.
- Close your eyes and concentrate on letting your breathing slow down naturally. Feel your whole body and mind steadying. Keep concentrating on the breathing and continue for at least another 5 minutes.
- For further help with this technique, ask a friend to work with you by reading all the above instructions in a quiet steady voice while you practise, counting the breaths with you and steadily slowing down the counting as you breathe.

Whether as emergency rescue from panic while you are waiting your turn outside the interview room, or as general preparation, this technique is hard to beat. Even five or six of these 7/11 breaths will produce instant positive results.

Classic self-relaxation

This approach starts in exactly the same way as 7/11 breathing though it is probably better if you are lying down rather than sitting. Some people find that a darkened room with some slow dreamy music and maybe a few candles can help get them in the mood. When you have found an easy, slow breathing pattern, you will work your way through each major muscle group:

● Picture yourself in a favourite quiet place: a beach, a mountain, a beauty spot, your favourite room at home. See yourself there, imagine how it feels, hear the sounds.
● Start with your feet. Unclench your toes and let them go floppy.
● Imagine a warm tingly glow of relaxation creeping up your legs. It will make the muscles soften.
● Let your knees flop apart.
● Your thighs should feel limp as if they are sinking into the bed or sofa.
● Feel your heart rate slowing right down in time with the breathing; concentrate on that for a few minutes and feel your chest and lungs opening out as they relax.
● Uncurl your fingers and let the softened feeling creep up your arms.
● Lower your shoulders and let go of any tension in them.
● Imagine that you are smoothing out any worry frowns and lines on your face until your face feels like a peaceful mask.
● Now start all over again and repeat three times.

The tapping treatment for managing intrusive thoughts

If worry about the interview has become an intrusive habit, try the so-called Tapping Treatment. The human imagination is so brilliant at its job that the brain cannot distinguish readily between the imagined thought and the real experience. This is why the emotion can feel overwhelming – it is just as if it is actually happening. This approach works when you are ruminating – i.e. indulging in persistent intrusive negative thoughts which become distressing, especially if they happen during a sleepless night. Sometimes presented as some kind of mysterious rite with talk of meridians, acupressure points and magnetic fields, technically it is most probably not so much the tapping, as the disciplined dissociation which does the trick. What you are doing is skilfully distracting yourself with a physical routine. Over a period of time, you are also dismantling habitual associations which maintain anxiety. However, if you prefer to believe that the tapping is some kind of magic – then feel free.

How to do it:

1. Summon up the ruminating thought – e.g. *I will fail at this interview, it will be awful*
2. Rate the thought on a 1–10 scale for intensity
3. Keep thinking about the negative thoughts while tapping beneath the collar bone with two fingers ten times
4. Tap under one eye with same two fingers ten times
5. Tap under your collar bone again ten times
6. Place your other hand in front of you and tap the back of it between your ring and little finger
7. Keeping your head still, keep tapping, while you look down right, look down left ten times each
8. Keep tapping; roll your eyes 360 degrees anti-clockwise, then clockwise – keep thinking about the negative thought
9. Hum *Happy Birthday* out loud and then hum it again
10. Check the ruminating on a 1–10 scale. Gone or very low? If not, repeat the whole cycle.

Visualizing success

Just as the human imagination can generate problems for us with its ability to create catastrophe in vivid colour, so it can also work for us positively. This technique works well for some people. In effect you are imagining yourself dealing with the interview in a wholly positive way.

- Set aside at least 15 minutes in a quiet place where you can guarantee no interruptions. Turn all your gadgets off.
- Start creating the interview scene in your head, a bit as if you are playing a DVD, fast-forwarding and pausing at a few key places.
- Imagine yourself coming into the room with poise, smiling, shaking hands and being welcomed by the panel.
- See yourself giving your presentation with panache and grace. The listeners are following intently, smiling warmly.
- Put yourself in the interview chair and watch yourself settling confidently into it, being eager to answer questions and pleased to be there.
- Imagine yourself answering some of the obvious questions fluently.
- See yourself leave the room feeling you have given an excellent account of yourself.

Variant: think back to a time when you faced a situation like an interview – or indeed an actual interview – and managed it with aplomb. Recall it in as much detail as you can: the sights, sounds, smells and feelings. Imagine yourself re-experiencing this scene. You should allow your whole system to become flooded by the pleasant associations. Imagine you're seeing it on a video screen, then freeze the scene at the moment of maximum impact. Practise recalling the scene several times before you go to the actual event. Then recall it again when you are tempted into nervousness.

These techniques are not exclusive options. You can try them all as a complete routine.

Blushing and wet hands

Blushing is more likely to be a problem for fair-skinned people in the sense that it is more visible, but it can affect anyone. Blushing is annoying to the blusher and it seems to be something of a puzzle. We are the only animals who blush and people of all races do it, but what purpose can it possible have when it is an out and out nuisance?

One suggestion is that it began as an appeasement signal – a sign of deference from a lower-status human to a higher-status one.

Whatever its evolutionary purpose, blushing is another common response to stress and happens when we feel embarrassed or socially disadvantaged. As with other responses to stress at interviews, the blusher can become preoccupied by the blushing, thus making it more likely to happen. At its worst, it can become a phobia with the sufferer avoiding any social situation. There are also some uncommon medical conditions that can involve blushing so it may be worth checking this out with your doctor. Women going through the menopause may find that any stressful situation can trigger embarrassing hot flushes. Despite what you may see on the internet with hundreds of eager hypnotherapists and 'NLP Practitioners' promising to take your money in order to get instant results, there are no easy cures. Here are some tactics that I have found can help some people:

- Accept that the blush is nothing like as noticeable as you may think. Some people do just have a ruddier complexion than others. A client of mine going through the menopause was haunted by the notion that she would get a hot flush during her interview. While we were practising some answers to typical questions she announced, 'Oh no! I'm having one now!' I peered at her but could see nothing except a little beading on her upper lip. Together we looked in a handy large mirror. She had to agree that although she felt burning hot, she showed little sign of it.
- Hypnotherapy may help. You can download free self-hypnosis audios from several sites on the internet so it may be worth giving that a try first. If you are contemplating employing a live hypnotherapist always look for a personal recommendation. Research seems to show that in about two thirds of cases, hypnotherapy works reasonably well for a wide range of anxiety and pain-control problems, but that still leaves about a third where it does not.
- All the self-calming tactics described above will help at least a little.

- Read the section on working a room on page 148. Blushing is a form of social phobia and the best cure for any phobia is to confront what you are afraid of.
- Stop trying to hide inside hugely high-necked sweaters or by growing your hair long enough for it to hide most of your face.
- Avoid alcohol and spicy food.
- Thick make up will just create the feeling that you have – well, thick make up on and is only open to women anyway. However, you can buy a green-tinted moisturiser/foundation that will cool down the appearance of reddened skin (green + red = beige). This may help to give you a little confidence.
- The best chance of improvement is to do something counter-intuitive. This is to embrace the blushing. The more you try to stop it, the worse it will get. Ask a trusted and respectful friend to work with you. The friend's role is to make you blush as often as possible. Just saying the words 'red' or 'blushing' may be enough at the beginning. Keep going. The friend should keep asking you to show them how easily you blush. You say, 'Yes, I can feel myself going red'. This does two things. First, you are gaining some control over something that feels uncontrollable, so if you can make yourself do it, you can learn to stop. Probably more important, it forces you to confront your fear and to see with the help of a sympathetic ally that the world does not end because you blush. So what? Most people redden a little when emotionally aroused and you can be emotionally aroused by joy or healthy anticipation as well as by fear. Think of the blushing as being about expressing excitement. You are keyed up – of course you are, so your face may become a little pinker than usual. Essentially, concern about blushing is about fear of exposure, and if you stop caring whether people see your fear, you will most probably find that the blushing reflex gradually fades away.

Wet hands: hyperhidrosis

A wet handshake is an embarrassment. People who suffer from it may sweat everywhere more than is normal and also be more inclined to blush. Shaking hands thus becomes a dreaded ritual. If it is mild, you can dry off your hands on a tissue just before going into the interview. Strong antiperspirants can also help.

Medical help

For severe cases of both facial blushing and hyperhidrosis, your doctor may be able to help, firstly by ruling out any underlying illness and secondly by recommending drugs such as porpanalol or clonidine. Where the blushing or hyperhidrosis is disabling, there is a surgical treatment called endoscopic thoracic sympathectomy (ETS) but this is a radical intervention and may cause as many problems as it solves. Hyperhidrosis can also be treated with Botox injections.

5 DRESSING THE PART

> **❝ Myth**: they need to take me as I am
>
> **Reality**: if you don't look the part, you won't get the job ❞

A few years ago I visited a client at her London headquarters for the first time. She ran a large team of mainly female buyers and managers for a fashion retail chain. As I crossed the busy open plan area which housed these people I realized that I was literally the only woman not to be wearing black, dark grey or deep navy. A few daring mavericks were wearing shirts in understated cream or oyster silk instead of the discreet black crew-neck sweater worn by the majority. I was wearing a jacket but it was in what suddenly felt like loud green and blue checks. My trousers were navy but I dislike high heels and my flat shoes now seemed like comfy old boats compared to the elegant high heels I saw all around me. The fact that my clothing was all well made and expensive did nothing to diminish my feelings of discomfort. I felt out of place. I asked my client whether her colleagues had been instructed to wear what looked like a uniform. She looked at me curiously, no doubt amazed at my naïvety. 'Oh no', she said, 'people in the fashion business just wear black all the time.' I made sure that on my next visit, I too was wearing a nice dark suit.

Human beings are tribal animals. We like and trust people who look and sound just like us. In our distant past as an emerging species we existed in tightly organized tribes of probably no more than 150 people. In the harsh struggle for existence it was no doubt important for us to be exquisitely tuned to who was 'one of us' and who was a dangerous stranger, to who looked 'normal' and who had some kind of difference that could make them a burden to the rest. Despite the equal opportunities legislation designed to make us behave better, we are still tribal to our core.

For the same reason we make instant judgements often on exceptionally flimsy data. It's no good bleating that we should not. The fact is that we do. All the greatest rogues and con artists, from bankers, politicians and evangelical preachers to dodgy lawyers and plain criminals in the business world know this, dressing in impeccably restrained suiting to impress us and to convey the message that we can trust them, even though it will turn out that this is the last thing we should have done. The worst of them are cynical actors, putting on a costume, all the better to deceive. As Scott Adam's anti-hero has it in Dogbert's Top Secret Management Handbook,

> *Clothes make the leader. Employees probably won't ever respect you as a person, but they might respect your clothes. Great leaders throughout history have understood this fact.*

So take it for granted that

> Most of us form an impression about others within a few seconds of meeting them.
>
> We form these impressions on the weak evidence of face, voice, clothes, age, body shape and smell long before we listen to the content of what someone has to say.
>
> These impressions are about whether someone is sexually attractive, their trustworthiness, values and morals, health, likeability, status and earning power – and much more.
>
> First impressions can be lasting and stereotyping inevitable.

Being appropriately dressed and groomed is therefore one of the easiest ways to ensure that you do not sabotage yourself within the first few minutes of a job interview.

In choosing what to wear for an interview you need to keep three principles in mind.

Principle 1

Dress as if you already have the job

This will mean reflecting a mirror image to the selectors, dressing exactly as they do.

This is especially important if you are going for promotion inside your existing organization. What do people already at that level of seniority wear? The custom here may be a lot more intricate than you realize. When I worked on a project with the now defunct but then powerful accountancy firm Arthur Andersen, one of the insiders kindly explained to me that there was a detailed if unspoken secret code about shirts for men. If you were ambitious, you never wore a shirt with a button down collar because partners wore hand made shirts with collars that sat perfectly in place without any need for buttons. If you couldn't afford a hand made shirt you bought an expensive off the peg shirt and pressed it carefully so that it looked as near as possible hand made. If you were American then a plain white or cream shirt was the only option. If you were European, then subdued stripes or subtle pastels were permissible. Proper double cuffs were essential: a buttoned cuff was a pitiable sign that you saw yourself as second rate.

Ask yourself how the dress of more senior people is different from what you currently wear. As soon as you aspire to a more senior job you should start wearing the appropriate dress, even if this raises eyebrows among your colleagues.

When I was hunting for my first managerial job I suddenly realized that women managers wore their own uniform. They didn't slop about in droopy floral dresses or parade in thigh-high skirts. They wore jackets with well cut skirts or trousers in darkish colours or else went for the Michelle Obama look with a tailored dress and cashmere cardigan. I borrowed some money from my parents and bought myself the same. I just felt different as soon as I put this stuff on – more of an authority figure though it caused some sarcastic comments from a few of my team mates.

If I had been going for a job at my client's company, it is unlikely that I would have got past a first informal interview. It would have been clear that either I had not bothered to research what people in the organization typically wore, or that if I had, I believed that somehow I was exempt from these informal, unstated, but nonetheless rigid rules. As an example, Gordon Brown, when Chancellor of the Exchequer, was notorious for refusing to conform to the white tie dress code when he addressed senior City of London business people at the annual Mansion House dinner. For many years he gave his speech as the only man in the room in a lounge suit. This caused amusement, puzzlement – and fury at his apparent rudeness. But who knows? Mr Brown does indeed have a reputation for prickly arrogance. When he did finally don white tie and tails it was at a state banquet where the dress code was laid down by the Queen. Mr Brown was absent from the entrance procession, tried to avoid being photographed and later appeared to hide behind a candelabra, so perhaps shyness is his problem. The point is that we cannot know his motivation and you cannot expect a potential employer to know yours if you breach the dress code. In the absence of information, employers come to their own conclusions.

> I was selecting for a very senior role, number three in the organization. It was largely an outward-facing job and the person would be expected to mix confidently with people at the same rank in other organizations. It was an internal appointment so we assumed people would understand the subtleties. We shortlisted one woman candidate. I was horrified at how she appeared at the interview: a cheap-looking suit in a bright royal blue with matching very high-heeled, obviously new, royal blue shoes, ill-fitting red blouse, hair all over the place, long dangly earrings. The only word for it was 'tarty'. It was embarrassing. And embarrassing all over again when I had to tell her she hadn't got the job, gave her some feedback about her dress and she threatened to take us to a tribunal because we were 'guilty of sexism' for criticizing her clothing! The fact was that no one would have taken her seriously wearing that stuff and I had to tell her that I thought it showed poor judgement on her part that she couldn't see this for herself.

Possibly this candidate thought that she was going to make an impression of vividness and daring by dressing as she did. She may have felt, as I have often heard from clients, 'I want to be different from all those grey men'. Sometimes it comes from defiance – this is how I am, so take it or leave it! Occasionally a take-me-as-I-am attitude is born from recklessness or from a wish to show the employer that the candidate is not going to play by the 'silly' rules of the interview game. This is a truly self-defeating tactic, guaranteeing that you will not get the job.

In general there is security in assuming that something formal will be safer than something less formal. But investigate first. Ask a friendly insider for advice on what to wear. In sectors such as media and advertising where people often pride themselves on their fashion sense or quirky eccentricity it may not impress if you turn up in a suit. Even here, however, beware of taking things to an extreme. For instance, jeans are rarely a sensible choice for a job interview as this male candidate discovered.

> I went for a job with a marketing team. In the informal interviews, I noticed that the men were all in jeans and T shirts. It looked casual but in fact that artless look took time and money. The jeans were Armani or Diesel and the T shirts expensive. Fortunately I asked the helpful HR person what she advised for the final interview. She suggested a well cut black suit with a dark polo shirt. I didn't have either but decided it was an investment in my future. It was a good idea because that was exactly what they wore. I felt immediately that I fitted in, the clothes gave me confidence – and I got the job!

Sometimes a strong candidate can get most of this right but then ruin a generally positive impact by adding some symbolic sign of allegiance. For instance I have seen all of these: club badges – e.g. Rotary, Women's Institute; club or old school ties; national flags worn as badges; AIDS and breast cancer ribbons; crucifix and fish (ichthus) symbols on badges and neck-chains; CND, gay or lesbian symbols as badges or earrings; Sikh bracelets; Star of David bracelets and necklaces; kippahs; garish charity bracelets. Don't do this, unless your adherence to your religion or cause outweighs everything else. The one exception might be wearing a poppy in November, but even this could have the power to annoy for the minority of people who believe in some perverse way that it glorifies war. The message you are sending when you wear symbols like this is: *see how deeply I care about my religion/political cause/gay identity!* As one employer said to me about a candidate whose left ear was decorated with a huge dangling lesbian emblem: 'I couldn't care less about her sexuality but it seems a bit pathetic to define yourself so one-dimensionally. I want a more rounded person.' You may disagree with such views, but this is how employers think. Organizations talk equality, multiculturalism and diversity but practise inequality, monoculturalism and conformity. This is obviously not good for them in the long term, but in the short term it gives the illusion of being beneficial because it makes reaching agreement quicker and easier.

Principle 2

Everything you wear should be in immaculately good condition

You are on show in a job interview from the moment you walk in to the moment you leave. If you look scruffy and unkempt, the assumption will be that the same is true of your thinking. If you can't be bothered to maintain order in your personal clothing, then you might treat work in the same way. If you are unaware of how your appearance strikes others then you may lack self-awareness generally, and self-awareness is essential for any job.

Never underestimate the level of scrutiny you will receive.

> I interviewed one candidate who had been a strong contender on the basis of her CV. As soon as she came into the room I thought, Oh no! We had deliberately gone for an informal set-up with no table. Throughout the 40 minutes she was there, I had ample time to observe the unrepaired hem of her creased skirt, the unpolished shoes with scuffed toes, the spreading sweat under her arms. Awful.

As part of your preparation, get out everything a week ahead, including shoes, bag or briefcase and other accessories that you propose to wear or carry. First do the sniff test. Clothing that has not been worn, laundered or dry cleaned for some time will smell musty even if it is clean. If you have stored wool or cashmere with mothproofing, it will smell strongly of whichever substance you have used. The smell will disappear if you hang the garment in fresh air for 24 hours. Subject everything to detailed inspection under the harshest, brightest light you can find. If you see food-blobs, splits, bobbles in sweaters, shiny areas where the nap of the fabric has worn away, scratches, scuffs, crumples, creases, scurf, make-up or sweat marks around the neck, sweat stains under arms, then launder, polish, repair, press, dry clean or replace the garment with something new. Now try the lot on, appraise yourself coolly, and see how it looks.

If you have gained or lost weight since the last time these clothes were worn, don't hope for the best.

> This candidate had a generous bosom and a too-tight shirt that left a gap in the middle. Try as I might, I kept staring at this gap. I could see a pink bra peeking out, very distracting. I kept imagining the button popping. I couldn't listen to what she was saying.

The gape and strain of a too-small shirt will also convey that you are unaware of your actual size and the baggy capaciousness of a too-large garment will make you seem small, shapeless and shrunken. Not good either way. Get the clothes altered by an expert or discard them and buy something that fits you better.

Principle 3

Dress for authority and high status

Whatever style statement you want to make, you will want to suggest the self-awareness and self-confidence that add up to an air of natural authority. The most important discriminator is therefore to choose high status rather than low status as your theme. Here are some guidelines suggested by my colleague Jennifer Aston, a specialist image coach:

Women

High status is suggested by	Low status is suggested by
Structured styles	**'Natural' styles**
These will have some tailoring, with at least some definite shape at the shoulders. Linings will help preserve shape. The underlying hint is of military uniform, i.e. an immediate authority symbol. All such uniforms are interlined and have squared shoulders.	Floppy, unstructured, loose clothing.
Definite colours	**Dressing to disappear**
But these should be the right colours for you: get advice on this. Big blocks of any one bright colour are not usually a good idea.	Please-don't-notice-me 'safe' and invisible colours, especially black or beige – these do not suit everyone.
Styled hair	**No-style hair**
Immaculately cut, conditioned and coloured.	Wash 'n' go appearance, e.g. wild curls, straggly or shapeless look, badly dyed or no thought to colour.
Light day make up	**No make up**
Women who wear discreet make-up look healthier and livelier. Research suggests that they get promoted far more often than women who don't.	All blemishes visible.
Keeping covered	**Stripping off**
	Bare legs, arms, cleavage, feet.
Looking contemporary	**Looking dull**
Note that this is not the same as being 'fashionable'.	Dressing as you did a decade or more ago.

High status is suggested by	Low status is suggested by
Immaculate grooming	Grubby grooming
	Clothes shiny from over-wear or urgently in need of dry cleaning/laundering. BO. Dandruff on collar, stains on tie.
Quality clothes in good condition	Shabby, poor-quality clothing
	Crumpled shirts, un-pressed trousers, frayed or curling collars.
Smart shoes, well polished	Shoddy shoes
	Shoes that look more suitable for leisure.
Elegant collar and tie	Distracting collar and tie
	In-your-face ties, knot too big or too small; collar wrong shape for face.
Up-to-date accessories	Yesterday's accessories

Some special tips on avoiding the low status look

Regardless of the sector or organization there are certain other things you should avoid at all costs.

Men	Women
Joke socks	Plunging necklines
Joke ties	Anything floral or with an animal print
Neck chains; huge signet rings, bracelets	Bare legs in open toed sandals
Unusual belts – e.g. with menacing symbols on the buckle	Top to toe bright colours – e.g. fuchsia, yellow, red
Sagging trousers which reveal underpants, especially if they have a designer name on the waistband	'Name' or 'initial' jewellery

Bow ties and cravats, even if meant 'ironically'	Sequins and glitter of any kind
Earrings; piercings	Dangling earrings, nose and lip studs
Pens in top pocket	Heavy make up; false eyelashes
Satchel worn across the chest	Hugely long nails whether real or false; bright nail varnish
Bitten nails	Bitten nails
Visible tattoo	Visible tattoo

Most of this is actually about middle class taste. So avoiding the low-status symbols may also mean avoiding the lower social status associated with appearing to be working class. This does not make it good or bad, only that if you want the job it is safer to appear middle class because it is largely middle class people who will be offering or withholding the job.

On the day

Smell control

As a young graduate I taught teenage boys and discovered their belief that deodorant was a substitute for washing, or even that if you sprayed deodorant onto your actual clothing, it would disguise smells. No wonder the classroom reeked of that instantly identifiable acrid smell of Lynx on an unwashed body. Amazingly some teenagers grow into men with the same habits and maybe there are even some soap averse women lurking out there. Laundering all your clothing, showering on the day of the interview and applying a good quality unperfumed deodorant will ensure that this is not your problem. If you have more than usually sweaty feet then consider investing in odour-absorbing insoles, as even with shoes firmly laced, heat can mean that smells leak out. If you smoke, get rid of those yellow stains on your fingers and use nicotine patches on the day of the interview. Many smokers have fooled themselves into pretending that there is no tobacco smell associated with smoking, but there is: it clings to clothing and hair. Anti-smoker prejudice is one of the few socially acceptable ways to openly express moral superiority and the merest whiff of tobacco could lose you the job.

> This candidate came into the room and an overpowering smell of stale smoke came in with him. Horrible. How could he not know? He'd obviously had one last fag moments before and his clothes were probably also permeated with it. I hate smoking. He didn't get the job – I ruled him out straight away.

Don't wear any perfume. Fragrance is a highly personal choice and what seems sophisticated and wonderful to you may seem sickly and overpowering to others in the room. It can carry the wrong message.

> I head up the buying function for the part of the business that handles accessories and beauty products so I was well clued up on fragrance. We were looking for an intern and someone I knew sent me her daughter, so out of courtesy I saw this girl. First she had horribly bitten finger nails, but far worse she was wearing <xxxx> a particularly nasty and expensive modern fragrance, with chocolaty top notes that I have always particularly disliked. It conveyed a take-me-or-leave-me impression and the room stank of it for hours afterwards. The fragrance is often bought by people who want to seem sophisticated but actually it shows how little taste they really have. She didn't impress me and the smell made me feel faintly sick.

Hair

Have a good haircut a week ahead just to allow for the cut to settle down. If you are male, make sure you trim ear and nasal hair. If five o'clock shadow is a problem for you, pack a battery-operated razor and give yourself a quick extra trim an hour ahead of the interview. Beards may also need radical trimming: anything suggestive of Father Christmas is not a good idea.

Long hair is potentially a problem for women, especially if it is fluffy, frizzy or curly. You may think the untamed look is attractive but it could say can't-be-bothered to an employer. Long straight blond hair may suggest Page 3 posing to some men (and women). But the real problem with long hair is that it looks girlish rather than grown up. There are some jobs where girlishness is an asset – for instance, lap dancing or working behind a bar, but looking girlish is at odds with looking authoritative. Giving the impression that you aspire to girlishness when you are over 40 may also suggest that you see yourself as cute or can't be trusted with real responsibility, because that's not what girls have. So consider pinning your hair up for the interview. This is extreme, but I had one client with thin, fine, blond, curly hair which she said was impossible to style. She had bought a good quality wig for interviews and other special occasions and had had it cut and styled into a beautiful bob.

Men's hair. Long hair on men is also a problem. No-nos include: ratty pony tails; comb-overs, wild curls, hair grown long at the back or sides to compensate for baldness at the front. Everyone sees through these disguises. Old fashioned styles such as the ice-cream cone look will suggest that you are old fashioned in your thinking. Hair colouring for men is a risk, especially clumsily applied black dyes or DIY blond streaks.

Untamed hair. When I do role-play rehearsals of job interviews with clients I frequently see women clients with bothersome deep fringes. They have delayed getting a hair cut and seem oblivious to the way they are constantly blinking away long bits of fringe that are literally getting in their eyes. Others have created messy hair for themselves, not the deliberately messed-up just-got-out-of-bed-with-a-lover hair that you see in fashion pictures, but accidentally messy: fronds that have fallen out of restraining clips and are now appearing behind ears or falling down necks. Again, the candidate may not notice how often she is twirling, stroking or pushing the offending strands out of the way. How this strikes an employer: first it is incredibly distracting, and then, if you can't restrain your hair what else might you not be able to restrain? So if you have the kind of fine hair which easily escapes, ask your hairdresser for advice on styles and products that will keep it in place.

Clothing

Give everything another close inspection. Run a lint-collecting roller over any dark clothing and if anything turns out to have blobs or stains, just replace it with something clean rather than dabbing and hoping for the best. If you have a long journey to the interview, consider packing your clothes carefully into a wheeled suitcase, or putting a suit into a suit carrier which you can drape over your arm to avoid creasing. Slip a traveller's sewing kit into your bag. Carry spares: for women, always have spare hosiery; for men, if you are wearing a tie, bring an alternative in case you drop food on to the one you plan to wear.

You may feel that you know all of this and that it is patronizing to have it pointed out. If so, then congratulate yourself on your wisdom. Dressing for the job does not win you the job, but if you are dressing in a way that suggests a poor fit, you will make it so much harder for yourself.

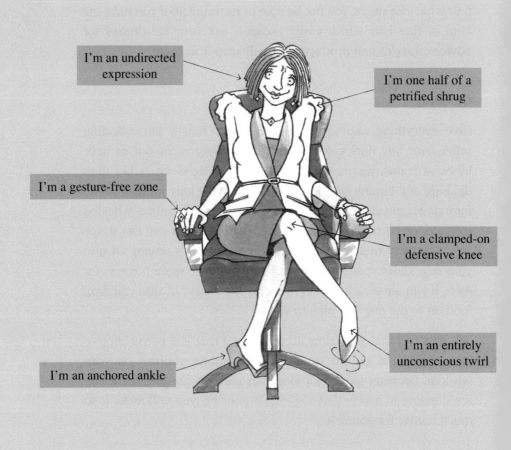

I'm an undirected expression

I'm one half of a petrified shrug

I'm a gesture-free zone

I'm a clamped-on defensive knee

I'm an anchored ankle

I'm an entirely unconscious twirl

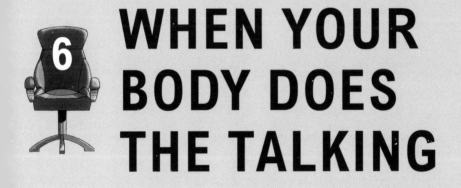

WHEN YOUR BODY DOES THE TALKING

> **Myth**: It's the words you use that matter in the interview
>
> **Reality**: The words do matter but so does how you handle the non-verbal communication

Like all other animals, we communicate our feelings through how we use our bodies. Although we congratulate ourselves on our superior consciousness, a great deal of this communication is not under our control because it happens outside awareness. If we are anxious, the fear can and will leak out in posture, facial expression and gesture. I have often seen so-called research quoted, claiming that x% (fill in the blank yourself, but make it large) of all communication is non-verbal. There is no such research, and if it were true then no one would ever need to learn a foreign language because we could communicate everything through gesture and facial expression alone. But the reason the myth of the research persists is because it is so plausible. It is certainly true that we do convey our feelings non-verbally. When you are going through a selection process for a job it is important to bring what you are unaware of into awareness and to manage as many of its negative aspects as you can.

Essentially it is about what is in your head. If you feel that you are at a chronic disadvantage in the interview, that you are going to be judged, interrogated, humiliated, scorned, rejected, then this belief could make failure more likely. When you know and believe that the interview is a meeting of equals and that you are choosing them as much as they are choosing you, many of the problems fade away.

The ideal: conveying relaxed authority

Most of the problems arising from body language come from feeling at a disadvantage and involve unconsciously demonstrating submissive behaviour. Occasionally I see the reverse problem – people who come across as arrogant, but this is rare.

Every employer wants someone like this: pleasant, socially adept, cheerful, confident, a good listener; a problem solver not a problem creator, easy work not hard work, low maintenance, not

93

high maintenance. The employer will judge how far you conform to this ideal by how you come into the room, how you shake hands, how you sit and what happens to your face and voice, as much as by what you actually say. Often the problem is that what is said and how it is said are at odds.

> I see many candidates who say the right words; e.g. that they are enthusiastic and committed but say these words in a drippy, squeaky voice while covering their mouths with their hands or turning away from me, or not doing good eye contact! I feel like saying, look at yourself! You don't fool me!

Handshakes

The purpose of the handshake is to create trust but how this is done varies enormously from one culture to another. For instance in some African countries, hands are held lightly, sometimes both hands for each person, for a period of minutes, while talking goes on apace. The French shake hands more frequently than the British, including with people they know well, whereas in the UK, we rarely shake hands with close friends and colleagues. Handshaking is more common between men than between women in most European countries. In some Arabic countries, men will not shake hands with women. Some cultures do not shake hands at all – they use bowing. In India they accompany this with the Namaste – palms lightly held together upwards in front of the heart. For purposes of this chapter, I am assuming UK custom.

Why handshakes matter

Your handshake is a vital part of creating the right first impression. It is the only opportunity the interviewers get to actually touch you. For something so fleeting, it can convey an enormous amount of information. For instance, if you offer your hand palm up, it conveys deference, inviting the other person to clamp down on it. Many women are totally unaware that they have developed a little curtseying dip as they shake hands, again conveying obedience or deference. The male equivalent is to do a mini-bow. One male client had got into the habit of merely touching the other person with the tips of his fingers and was amazed to hear that this conveyed acute distaste for the hand-shaking partner. A man applying for an extremely senior government job leant backwards, held his arm out stiffly so that it looked like a weapon – and combined this with looking straight over my shoulder, avoiding all eye contact, in his practice handshake. Few of my clients have ever had feedback on their handshakes and maybe half of them, all sensible people, do turn out to have problems here.

The wrong impression

The boneless	*No grip. Conveys lack of confidence.* *Better: brief squeeze of the other person's hand*
The seducer	*Holds on too long. Conveys sexual interest.* *Better: don't do it in a business context*
The patronizer	*Clasps the other person's hand in both of theirs. Conveys fatal over-familiarity* *Better: don't do it. One hand is enough*
The dominator	*Forces their hand on yours from above. Conveys potential bully* *Better: make sure your hand meets the other person's hand sideways on*
The pixie	*Barely touches; hand flutters. Conveys lack of seriousness. Often accompanied by lack of eye contact* *Better: as for boneless*
The one-arm bandit	*Whole arm extends stiffly. Conveys that they feel threatened, or worse, that they feel superior* *Better: keep the arm relaxed*
The cruncher	*The other person's hand hurts afterwards* *Better: use 50% less force than you first thought of*
Wet hand	*See page 71*

95

Wherever possible, arrange to leave your coat and any other belongings in a secure place so that you enter the interview arena uncluttered. Ideally you should be carrying just one bag in your left hand – a smart briefcase or laptop bag. This leaves your right hand free for the handshake. Approach the handshake with your mind on the other person and aiming to convey how genuinely pleased you are to meet them. There is often a practical problem with a large panel of people. If there are more than four people, it becomes impractical to shake hands with all of them, but if they initiate it, then approach each one confidently.

The ideal handshake – conveys equality and confidence

- If you are sitting in a waiting area and the interviewer approaches, always stand up – remaining seated looks rude, as if you believe you are too grand to stand up
- Wait for the interviewer to offer their hand; they are on their territory so they should initiate the handshake
- Step towards the person confidently and facing frontwards, not too close, not too far away
- Smile using your eyes as well as your mouth
- Keep your arm relaxed
- Make direct eye contact and hold it for the whole handshake
- Your hand and the other person's hand meet web-to-web (i.e. thumb to thumb) sideways on
- Give the other person's hand a brief squeeze – not too gentle, not too strong
- Give one pump, or two at the most

It's all very well to read this list, but it will not give you feedback as you cannot shake your own hand. So my advice is to enrol a frank friend. Practise coming into the room, offering your hand and then shaking the friend's hand. Listen carefully and undefensively to what they say. Practise it until the friend is satisfied that you have got it right.

Entering the room

You may have to do this innumerable times during the selection process – for instance at each phase of an assessment centre – but you will always have to do it for the panel interview. Do a last minute appearance check in front of a full-length mirror before you are called. For men: flies fastened, cuffs secured, tie in place? For women: do a hair, lipstick and make up check (e.g. hair in place, no lipstick on teeth or smudged mascara). For both sexes, jackets should be buttoned. You can undo the buttons once you are sitting down. A buttoned jacket makes you look literally more together. You will be ushered into the room but may have to enter it alone if, for instance, you are being brought in by a PA. Have your smile ready before the door is opened and enter the room full on – no sideways sliding or over-modest ducking. Enter with dignity and alertness, walking tall. Take your time to look around the room, engaging each person with eye contact, a smile and a brief greeting. Wait to be asked to sit and, if it is unclear which seat you are expected to occupy, ask.

Sitting

Sitting down is a three-stage process: feeling the edge of the seat with the back of your thighs and grasping the arms with your hands, sitting against the edge of the chair and then easing your bottom into the back of it.

There is really only one way to sit at a job interview and that is with your bottom tucked snugly into the back of the chair, sitting upright but not rigid with your feet firmly planted side by side on the ground and your shoulders relaxed. When nervous, we betray our anxiety by perching on the edge of the chair and leaning forward, or else show that we might really like to disappear by hunching, half-turning away and trying to make ourselves seem small or letting our feet tap. Crossing arms, often interpreted as a sign of defensiveness, which it sometimes is, is more probably a sign of wanting to disappear in a job interview, though the basic instinct is no doubt the same – wanting to protect yourself.

Sometimes the interview chairs will make it a challenge to sit comfortably and confidently. For instance, I attended some interviews as the external assessor in a smart modern office with 'designer' chairs. Whichever designer was responsible for them should have been punished by being obliged to sit in them, as we were, for a whole day. No candidate could be comfortable, any more than we could – you either sank deep into the low, womblike enclosure of the chair or perched on its unforgiving hard edge. If you chose the womb-option, you then had to struggle, legs waving helplessly, to get out again. Plan for this by making sure that your clothing will take the deep, low chair test. If female and planning to wear a skirt, are you still decent, or does your skirt ride up exposing a lot of thigh, or even worse, crotch? If male, do your trousers cover your shins?

Never wind your legs around the back of the chair, or twist your legs around each other. In fact even crossing your legs can look over-relaxed and it's a definite no-no to sling one leg over the thigh of the other. It's better to keep feet firmly planted on the ground. If you're male, don't do too much of that man thing where you spread your knees wide – it looks aggressive and will remind every woman in the room of the boorish males, unfortunately met on every tube and bus, who seem unaware that they are taking up most of a double seat by sitting like this.

It can be hard to remember advice about keeping your shoulders down, sitting up though not too rigidly, not twiddling your feet – and so on. The best way to do this is to concentrate on a powerful muscle called the transversus abdominis. This is the body's natural corset and it runs almost all the way around your midriff. If you now put a hand on your belly, pulling it inwards in an attempt to flatten it, you will feel this muscle engage. Doing so stabilizes your spine. When you engage this muscle you will automatically sit up looking alert but relaxed and your shoulders will most probably also relax. You will look natural, not rigid as though someone has filled you with cement by accident. Because the transversus abdominis is also attached to the diaphragm your lungs will get the chance to expand, which will aid correct breathing. So all in all, this is a brilliant way to ensure comfortable, confident-looking posture while sitting, easy breathing and plenty of volume and projection to your voice. I recommend that you give this muscle plenty of practice for up to 20 times a day well in advance of the interview so that you can get it to do its work instantly, even in the excitement of the interview.

Managing common problems

What to do with your hands

Hands can seem to have a life of their own: getting sweaty, fluttering nervously, plucking at invisible fluff on your clothing, touching your face, waving themselves about, tapping the table. All of these gestures convey: *I don't believe in myself.* Beware especially of touching your face or fiddling with your hair. One of my clients had the habit of rotating one of her expensive diamond stud earrings like a dial. The real meaning of the gesture was 'I need time to think about this', but it conveyed uncertainty. These can be self-soothing gestures: an unconscious impulse to calm yourself down. Covering your mouth with a hand can suggest that you don't really have faith in what you are saying. For men there are additional traps. Running a hand around the inside of your shirt collar conveys, 'I am getting hot under the collar' which may of course be literally as well as metaphorically true. Adjusting and then stroking a tie can sometimes look like a sexual come-on to a female interviewer. I once saw an astonishingly unaware candidate lean back in his chair, stroke his tie vigorously, lift his hands above his head, give a good stretch, spread his legs, while pointing his groin at the attractive young woman interviewing him. She was not impressed with this bravura display of male potency. He did not get the job.

Cure

The cure is all about self-discipline and practice. One of the first techniques that student actors learn is to manage their hands and arms by letting them lie in a curving line along skirt or trouser seams, with the hands held loosely like a bunch of bananas. Try this and see how it feels and then practise it. That's fine for standing up. For sitting down, practise putting your hands loosely on your lap or lightly on the table in front of you. They should not be rigid as that, too, will convey tension. For several days before the interview, practise this at every meeting whether social or professional until it becomes second nature. If you use gestures for emphasis (a good idea) make them slow, deliberate and steady.

Face

Glasses need managing. If you wear them all the time this is probably less of an issue than occasional wear for reading. Nervousness can lead to fidgeting with glasses or to whipping them on and off. However, the real killer is looking over their upper edges. This comes across as patronizing and critical. If you have the habit of looking over the top of your glasses you probably need varifocals or at the very least a better-fitting pair. Contact lenses solve this problem entirely for short-sighted people. People need to see your eyes, so never wear the kinds of lenses that darken in bright light. At worst these look sinister, at best pretentious.

Ideally you need a pleasant, open, smiley face. *Smiley* means smiling a lot of the time, not an unconvincing, fixed grin but a pleasant, spontaneous response to answering questions from someone you might enjoy working with. A warm, natural smile especially one given at the beginnings of your answers will help a lot.

I find that many of my clients are unaware that they frown a great deal. Unacknowledged short sight is one cause, but a habit of frowning while concentrating is probably the most common. Sometimes people have a hearing problem and pucker their brows while they are straining to understand a person with a quiet voice. Unfortunately, in a job interview, frowning looks like disapproval – people cannot read your mind, they do not know what your motivation is. You may be thinking, 'I need to concentrate to understand this question' while the interviewer is thinking, 'What on earth is this woman scowling at me for?' Look at your forehead now. If you have deeper lines between your eyebrows than is normal for your age you probably frown a lot. Other negative habits that may need managing include chewing, twisting or licking your lips or turning your mouth down while thinking.

Eye contact is important. While Person A is asking their question, it's easy to be seduced into thinking that all you need to do is to engage Person A in eye contact. Not so. You are actually addressing the entire panel and need to sweep the room with your eyes when you answer any individual question. The give-away is when you see one of the panel looking down, scribbling notes. If they are scribbling, they cannot be giving you their full attention. Make a deliberate effort to regain it by aiming your voice in their direction and seeking eye contact with them. That usually succeeds. Don't stare – it is disconcerting and looks aggressive. Don't close your eyes: this may seem obvious but people do it at an unconscious level as a way of protecting their privacy while they think. If you have this habit, give it up.

Leaving

The selectors or assessors will begin to give you signals that the session is over – for instance, tapping their papers into a neat pile, looking at watches, changing their posture. Be alert to all of these – like any thoughtful guest, you do not want to outstay your welcome. Never spoil your exit with a clumsy handshake-lean: this is the one where in your haste to get out of the room, you forget that you have a lap full of papers, or a glass of water on the table in front of you and desperately semi-fall across the table to shake hands, scattering everything as you do so.

Gather your things together swiftly but steadily. If they offer to shake hands again, do so gracefully. Give each person a smile and some eye contact, taking your time as you stand up. Thank them for seeing you and exit cleanly.

101

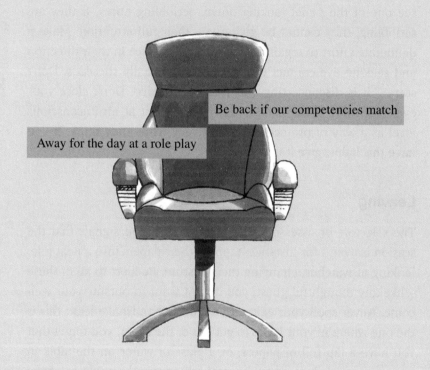

7 ASSESSMENT CENTRES

> **Myth**: assessment centres are another way employers torment candidates
>
> **Reality**: they are enjoyable and increase the chances that the best person will be appointed

The closer a selection method can replicate the demands of the actual job the better. Research repeatedly shows that the more data you have about a candidate, the better the quality of the decision – and one way you get more data is to run an assessment centre.

What is an assessment centre?

This way of choosing people started in Germany between the two world wars when the German army began running observed exercises to select officers. It was taken up by the British army in 1942: war had revealed that traditional methods of choosing officers were based on such flimsy factors as 'exceptional smartness' and that the actual criteria for becoming an officer were the narrow ones of educational and social background. The Office of Strategic Studies in the US used assessment centres to select spies, also during the Second World War. The method was taken up by US companies after the war, notably by the giant AT&T. Now it is a respected and widespread way of appointing staff. In fact you should be reassured if the employer has commissioned an assessment centre. It absorbs considerable resources in time, people and money and is a sign of the employer's commitment to making the best possible choice.

An assessment centre is a process, not a place. It may last anything from half a day to three days or more. What happens is that you will be asked to take part in a variety of exercises which simulate the skills and behaviours that will be needed in the job. The panel interview may happen as just one part of the centre, as a totally separate event, or as the final phase. Assessment centres are based on the well researched assumption that the best way to predict future performance is to see how people carry out tasks that are similar to those they will need in the job. You will be observed against a checklist of ideal behaviours during every stage of the centre. After the candidates have left, the assessors get together to compare their views and agree who should be offered a job.

Typically, assessment centres are used for jobs where the employer is taking in large numbers of new staff at any one time. This makes it easier to justify the costs, so centres are commonly used for graduate entrant schemes and also for jobs where there is a high degree of churn – for instance in call centres or telesales. Centres are also used for individual senior jobs where the cost of making the wrong decision is enormous.

A well designed assessment centre is fairer and more sensible than just relying on a panel interview because

- It is based on a careful analysis of the skills needed for the job
- Decisions are based on seeing your actual behaviour rather than just listening to you make claims in self-flattering terms
- The focus is on what the job will need in the future, not on how it was done in the past
- It involves the independent judgement of several assessors, so 'group-think' or a panel being swayed by one powerful voice is far less common
- It relaxes candidates: it is hard to remain at a high level of nervousness during a whole day
- Even if you are not successful as a candidate, you are far more likely to feel that you have had a fair chance to show what you can do
- Candidates benefit from a clearer understanding of what the job will involve and, if rejected, are more likely to understand why
- A good employer will offer feedback for all candidates so there is a developmental aspect to the process.

What will happen

You will be greeted by the 'Centre Manager' – often one of the HR team – who will show you your timetable for the day. It will be a series of activities, typically around an hour to 90 minutes each with periods for rest or preparation in between. There will be a room set aside for candidates, with tea, coffee and water available all day. If there is anything bothering you or information that you feel you lack at this stage, this is the time and the person to ask.

A warning

You are being assessed the entire time you are on the premises. This applies to selection processes that are just an interview as well as to assessment centres. It also applies to the views of people who have no formal voice in the process, such as reception and admin staff. Be rude or careless with them at your peril.

> I always ask my PA what she thinks of the candidates. She meets them at Reception and looks after them while they wait, offering them tea, showing them where the loo is and so on. She is amazingly insightful and I am always aghast at how readily some people seem to assume they can behave any way they like with her as she is 'only' a PA. She will comment to me later on how organized they seem, whether they are polite to her, how far they are able to make small talk with her, do they seem demanding and difficult, how well they manage their nerves – and so on. She's rarely been wrong in her judgements!

Competencies and their role in assessment centres

The off-putting word *competency* has an important role in a robust selection process. A competency defines the knowledge, skills, abilities and personal characteristics needed to do the job. This is much more helpful to selectors and candidates than just listing the tasks that the job is likely to involve. The employer should tell you in advance what competencies they are looking for. If an assessment centre is well run, they will also tell you which exercises are designed to judge which competencies. Normally in any one

107

exercise the observers will be looking out for two or three such competencies.

Let's assume that the competency is team-working, something that is needed in almost all jobs at any level in an organization. You will be invited to take part in an exercise which involves teamwork. The assessor might have a mark sheet like this

Name of candidate	
Competency: team-working	**Ability to work collaboratively with others towards a common goal**
Positive indicators	*Evidence*
Contributions focused on group task	
Listened attentively	
Contributed enthusiastically	
Helped others contribute	
Showed sensitivity to others' feelings	
Negative indicators	*Evidence*
Over-contributed	
Interrupted or put down others	
Showed insensitivity to others' feelings	
Sulked, argued or withdrew when ideas rejected	

Some of these assessment sheets might also involve marks out of ten.

Types of assessment centre activity

There are dozens of possible types of exercise: role plays; personality questionnaires; 'games' – for instance to build something as part of a team; ability and aptitude tests; written exercises such as case studies from which you have to recommend a plan of action; in-tray exercises which simulate a typical manager's email box; technical interviews which test your subject knowledge; discussion based exercises, usually with other candidates; presentations; fact finding and analytical exercises; simulations and a competency based interview.

It would be impossible to cover all of these in a short chapter so I have concentrated on the most common, which are also the ones that employers find cheapest and simplest to run.

Psychometrics

Psychometric means literally *measuring the mind*. There are thousands of such tests, some of poor quality. The best are based on many years of skilled research, developing and improving the test through trying it out on large samples of people. To buy such tests you must be trained and licensed.

Despite their appearance of scientific magic and secrets, psychometrics play a relatively minor part in selection decisions. The output of questionnaires is mainly useful for eliminating what a colleague once dubbed 'the obvious crazies' and most of us are boringly within normal spectrums. It would be very rare indeed for a questionnaire result to be used as a reason for not appointing, or indeed for appointing a candidate. Sensible test administrators, even the greatest fans of these questionnaires, know that they are only indicators, not god-given truths.

The questionnaire report will raise issues that should be probed at interview, allowing you to answer for yourself. A typical example of such a question might be

> *So, X, in completing your personality questionnaire, it was suggested that you like to involve others in decision making but also that you rather like having your own way! How true would you say this is?*

Then depending on the reply, a follow up question might be

So how do you reconcile these two needs? Can you give us an example?

Personality questionnaires

A personality questionnaire is a series of carefully designed questions which enable you and the employer to see how your personality might fit or get in the way of the job the employer wants to fill. These questionnaires are commonly known as 'tests', though since they do not have right/wrong answers they are not strictly speaking tests. Human personality has been studied as a science for over 70 years with repeated attempts to find a holy grail of factors which can easily be measured. You are most likely to encounter *trait-based questionnaires* at assessment centres, where the questionnaire will measure, often on a scale of 1–10, how much or how little of a trait you believe you have.

One consensus that has emerged is that there are five predominant factors with their associated traits in human personality. They are

- Agreeableness: how far you are concerned with social harmony and the wish to be liked, putting effort into getting on with others
- Conscientiousness: How far you show self-discipline, act dutifully, and aim for achievement; planned rather than spontaneous behaviour
- Extraversion: how far you have a tendency to seek the stimulation and company of others
- Neuroticism: how far you seem emotionally stable, for instance how you respond in a crisis
- Openness: how far you hold unconventional and individualistic beliefs and are open to new experiences

Many of the leading test publishers now have questionnaires that probe these areas. Note that although you may conclude when reading about these factors that it is 'obvious' what the 'right' answer should be, actually it is not. For instance, you could score at either extreme of the Agreeableness spectrum. At one end you might be overly concerned with what others think, which could make it difficult for you to deal with conflict. At the other, you might be indifferent, leading to ignoring people's views at times when you should be taking notice.

After you complete the questionnaire, which may be done in advance and online, the administrator will be able to print off a computer generated report. You should eventually be given a copy of this – if you are not, you should ask for it.

Dealing with personality questionnaires

- Note that this is a self-assessment so is potentially prone to the distortion of answering either as you would secretly like to be or how you imagine the employer sees the ideal employee. Second guessing what the employer wants is bound to be wrong. Just be yourself. Don't ponder too much. Answer instinctively.
- The best questionnaires ask repeated, cunningly designed versions of the same areas to check the consistency of your answers. They may also have 'lie detectors', known in the trade as 'faking good' questions. This is where the test developers know that people may believe for instance that in general extraversion is considered to be 'better' than introversion (please note that, speaking as an introvert myself, it is not), so will plant apparently innocent questions which tempt you to put yourself in the best light in an unrealistic way. So for instance, if you encounter a question inviting you agree with the statement that you never lie, you should resist. Everyone lies sometimes. Agreeing will simply cast doubt on many of your other scores.
- A good questionnaire has extremely subtle items and scoring. You will find it difficult to know which factors any individual item is assessing let alone being able to guess how it is scored.
- Answer all the questions.
- There is usually no time limit on these questionnaires but guide times for finishing are usually given. If after an hour you are still

111

plodding through a questionnaire where the normal time for completion is 40 minutes, an employer might well raise questions about whether you would also be agonizingly slow in your work or else just chronically unsure about who you really are.

● If you are invited to complete the test online at home, never, ever, ask someone else to do it for you. It will be immediately obvious that the person the assessors see at the centre is not the same as the person who completed the test. You may then be asked to take the test again, this time under invigilated conditions – that is if the employer has not already excluded you for cheating.

Ability and aptitude tests

These genuinely are tests because they have right/wrong answers. Tests have come a long way since the crudities of the original 'IQ' tests, which depended as much on general knowledge and therefore on class, nationality and education as on any innate intelligence. Now there are tests which assess verbal reasoning, numerical reasoning, spatial ability, manual dexterity, spelling – and many others. The most commonly used are verbal reasoning – a test of your ability to use logic to justify a conclusion – and numerical reasoning. There are different tests for different levels of seniority.

People often ask if coaching or practice will improve their likely scores. Yes, it can, especially for numerical reasoning tests, sometimes by a significant amount, depending on the test and on your innate abilities. So if you are sent a practice test in advance you should definitely study it carefully to see if you can understand its internal logic and what exactly it is testing. Puzzles like Sudoku, which rely on pure logic, can boost skill and confidence for verbal reasoning tests. You can try psychometric tests free on the internet, though it is unlikely that you will find one that is identical to the one the employer has chosen, as the publishers guard their copyright fiercely. You can also buy books which give sample tests of all sorts and there will probably be some examples which resemble the type of test you will be taking. All of this practice is useful.

112

There are two types of test: speed tests, where questions at the same level of difficulty have to be completed within a set time; power tests, which allow more time and contain progressively more difficult questions and where the quality of your answers is under scrutiny. For practice at speed tests, set a kitchen timer and try the test within the time limits. Online tests will do this for you.

Some people have hang-ups about maths and become anxious about taking numerical reasoning tests. Many such tests are really just arithmetical sums or else exercises in logic and few go beyond GCSE maths. However, you may have forgotten principles you once knew well, so remind yourself of all of the following: multiplication and division, ratios, percentages, fractions, decimals, probability, negative numbers and simple algebra. The BBC's website has a section devoted to skill-building in maths: bbc.co.uk/skillswise/numbers. There is a little known condition called dyscalculia, most probably a developmental disorder, which makes arithmetical tests difficult for a minority of people. People who have it may also have problems with time, spatial reasoning and measurement generally. If this is diagnosed for you, you will need to let the centre manager know, as you will if you have dyslexia.

Other hints

- If you know you will feel nervous during this part of the centre, read and re-read the section on managing nervousness (chapter 4).
- Just as you were told at school when taking written exams, it is vital to read the instructions carefully. It is helpful that there is always a worked example.
- Read every question carefully. For instance, with verbal reasoning tests, the answer is always in the material you are given and the test is an exercise in pure logic. Normally these are multiple choice questions. Take each possible answer in turn and ask yourself: is this possible conclusion justified by the evidence I have? NEVER, EVER GUESS.

- Work out how many questions there are for the time available. So for instance, the Watson-Glaser, the gold standard of verbal reasoning tests, has 80 questions and you have a strictly timed 40 minutes to answer. This means that you have 30 seconds for each answer. Keep scanning the time to see how you are doing. After 20 minutes, you should be half way through.
- Deal with questions you can answer straight away first and come back to the more difficult ones later.
- With most timed tests you get no credit for working accurately but super-slowly. So if you completed all 40 of the items you tackled correctly but left 40 unanswered, your score will be the same as that of a person who tried 80 but only got 40 right.
- Take in your own pen, pencils, pencil sharpener and eraser. If the instructions specify using a pencil, do so.

Role plays

This is what happens. You will be given a brief to study, with plenty of time to absorb it. It may be sent to you in advance. The scenario will describe a situation which is commonly encountered in the job for which you are applying. The focus is always on conflict or persuasion of some kind – for instance, a poorly performing colleague or an unhappy customer. Your role will be to deal with the difficulty in a way which sorts the problem out and ideally leaves both parties with their self-respect intact. You play yourself and are not required to do any more than behave as you would normally. The other party may be played by a professional actor. Sometimes the conversation will be videoed. You should be told which competencies are being assessed; if not, ask.

Role play is an excellent way of seeing how you cope with the parts of the job that involve dealing with people. You say in your application that you are brilliant at dealing with customers, but are you? You might be good by your own standards, but do you meet ours? You claim success at sales, but how do you handle a prospective customer at a first meeting? You describe negotiating with suppliers but do you really get a good price in a way that preserves the relationship? Even though it is true that the situation is artificial, enough of the candidate's normal style is still clearly visible.

Hints on doing well at role play

- You are not required to act – any acting will be done by the other party. The actor will be briefed to respond to your behaviour, so although there will be an outline script, the actor will improvise, will have been told to follow their instincts about how to play out most of the scene and will have licence to respond to your behaviour.
- Assume that you are showing the assessor how you normally deal with situations like the one being played out. Don't smirk, don't try a comedy turn or assume some other kind of stagey personality. Be yourself.
- Read the brief carefully, especially the part which tells you what outcome is expected ideally from the conversation. Use the planning time fully – something that I have noticed many candidates fail to do: instead they quickly scan the brief and then stare vacantly around the room or pace about nervously. Think: what might the underlying issues be here? How is the role player likely to behave? How should I open the meeting? What information should I be seeking?
- Take a little time at the beginning to create some rapport with the other person. Spend a few minutes agreeing what a good outcome would be for both sides, then a few minutes more on how you will spend the time and re-confirming what time is actually available. Listen when the role player expresses a view. Often they will display anger or other emotional extremes. React calmly and summarize their opinions before offering your own.
- The role play will be planned so that the actor resists something that you have been instructed to achieve as part of your brief. Handle this by enquiring into their objections courteously, summarizing again and then making your own suggestions about how to resolve the difficulty.
- It would be common for the actor to have been told to keep back some vital information which could affect the whole

scenario. For instance, if the actor is playing a supplier who is resistant to ideas about improving quality, he or she may have as part of their brief that their company is about to be merged, and that this is why they cannot make immediate changes in production. This may only be disclosed if you spot the right signs – for instance, hesitancy, looking down, frowning, looking upset – followed by you asking the right questions. A good all-purpose question to keep up your sleeve here is, 'I wonder if there's anything else that it would help me to know here?' and then just wait patiently for the reply.

It is worth putting effort into the role play as it is highly influential in making decisions about candidates.

Group exercises

These exercises are designed to assess competencies such as team-working (see page 108). So the assessors will be looking at how well you listen, how clearly you put a point of view, how respectful you are to others in the group. You will be in a group with four or five other candidates and asked to complete a task with strict time limits, rarely more than 40 minutes. There are two possible variants:

You are given a topic to discuss and asked to make a decision or recommendation by the end of that time.

You are given some raw materials and told to make some kind of object, for instance a tower from Lego or a 'toy' from paper and string.

No leader will be appointed. There will be at least two assessors in the room and they will take no part in the discussion other than explaining the task at the outset.

The challenges

You are working with other candidates – your competitors – so it can feel like a sacrifice to behave in a way that might give them an advantage. Then there is the whole question of whether you are supposed to lead the group or just take part. Should you speak a lot or a little? Remind yourself about what is being assessed: usually it is team-working or influencing. The overriding issue is therefore how much effort you are prepared to put into setting personal interests aside for the sake of a common goal.

> This guy was on paper the ideal candidate. He had already held a similar job to the one that was now available, presented himself confidently and gave every impression that he was a shoe-in for the job. Everything went fine for him until the group exercise. He offered himself as the leader and did a lot of talking about how he thought the group should work. He became more and more bombastic and after about five minutes of this, the group started to disagree and told him they didn't like his ideas. At first he just stepped up the bombast, but then they began excluding him. He suddenly leaned back, pushed his chair away from the table, caught my eye as one of the assessors, winked, shrugged, rolled his eyes, folded his arms and took no further part in the exercise. That was him finished as a candidate. He'd shown us so clearly how little he was able to tolerate disagreement. If he couldn't be the boss, he didn't want to play!

It is equally disastrous to shrink modestly into yourself, to mumble or leave all the talking to the others. The ideal is to contribute fully without dominating.

However, your best tactic is to do something which few candidates ever do, and that is to position yourself as the person who can help the group with its *process* rather than just treating it at the level of the task and subject. This means seeing yourself as a facilitator as well as someone taking part in the discussion. The reason this matters is that virtually all candidates taking part in group discussions want to plunge straight into the task – they are anxious to show what they can do, get gripped by the topic, and want to impress the assessors. What then follows is at least five minutes, often more, of chaos as group members tumble over each other offering rival ideas. No one is listening to anyone else and in effect people are just queuing to speak.

This is what you should do.

Interrupt the discussion at the earliest possible stage and say, *I think it would help us to agree how we're going to work. For instance, should we elect a chair? And how about other roles like time-keeper? Should we use the flip-chart?* This is usually enough to focus the other group members. Then as the discussion goes along, take opportunities to summarize what other people have said, without using it as a chance to put forward your own views (you can do this separately). So you might say, 'so we seem to have a range of views here, X has said this, Y has said that . . .' Or you can notice that there is one person in the group who has yet to contribute: 'I notice Z hasn't spoken for a while and I'm wondering if there's anything she wants to say . . .'

Other hints

- The more effort you have put into getting to know the other candidates during breaks or in other exercises, the easier the group activity will be. Everyone is likely to be feeling at least a little nervous. Ask them about what they are currently doing; aim to put them at their ease.
- Use people's names but don't over-use them because it can seem manipulative.
- Get into the discussion early. The longer you leave it to make your first point, the harder it will be to contribute later.
- When you are speaking, smile, keep your head up and look around the room engaging each person in brief eye contact.
- If you are challenged outright by someone in the group, stay calm and do what virtually no one does in these circumstances: *invite the person to say more.* For instance, 'That's an interesting point, Z, talk me through how you got to that conclusion . . .'

- If your pet idea is rejected by the group, just live with it graciously – don't mope or get angry and upset.
- You can give yourself an important advantage in advance. Where you know or suspect that there is to be a group exercise, ask a friendly colleague from your current organization to watch you in a meeting and to offer you private feedback at the end about how you came across. This will give you a level of self-awareness that the other candidates may not have.

> The woman who won the job looked mousy at first and almost didn't make the short-list because she seemed inexperienced, but she shone in the group exercise. Whereas the other four just leapt in and started arguing about why their particular idea was wonderful, she stayed steady, very confident in a quiet way, pointing out that they would get nowhere until they had planned their time properly. They all looked a bit sheepish. She proposed that they spend five minutes discussing how to generate ideas, then another ten on agreeing the benchmarks for making a good decision and the final ten minutes on making the decision. Of course they tried to go off track but she reminded them of their agreement. It was impressive. I remember thinking, Wow! This would be one useful person to have in my team.

Assessment centres: general advice

- Have a decent breakfast: if you skip this meal your concentration and energy will for certain be impaired. Plan your journey to the centre and allow more time than you think you need. If you are late, the centre manager will not let you participate because the timetable is so tightly planned. Charge your phone, make sure it contains all the contact details you need and is turned off during the exercises. Bring any paperwork that has been sent to you along with your CV and application. Remember to bring writing implements, glasses, business cards, tissues and a bottle of water and put all of this in a professional-looking bag – this is not the time for improvising with a Sainsbury's Bag for Life.

- Be aware that you are on show the whole time and this includes how you treat everyone you meet. Be courteous and friendly at all times.
- Look after your own well-being. Take a brief walk during the lunch break if there is time.
- Go to the lavatory and empty your bladder before you start any new part of the centre, even if you feel you don't need to.
- Don't allow feelings about having 'failed' at any one activity upset you while you tackle the next. Although some activities undoubtedly have more weight than others, you have the whole centre to show what you can do and few people do brilliantly at all of the activities.
- Use the preparation time between activities to the full.
- Don't use your mobile at all during the centre unless you are actually outside the building and totally unobserved. It will distract you and look self-important.

8 GIVING THE PRESENTATION

> **❝ Myth**: the presentation at a job interview is about the brilliance of your thinking
>
> **Reality**: the presentation is about your ability to communicate and persuade **❞**

The more senior the job, the more likely it is that you will be asked to make a presentation as part of the selection process. The most common place for this to happen is in the first 15 minutes of the panel interview where the panel are therefore your audience, but if there is an assessment centre it can also be designed into this day. Your nervousness or confidence about the presentation may depend on how often you have to give presentations in your current or previous job. If it is a routine part of your work you may have long since overcome any anxiety. If you have never given a presentation before then it may create feelings of dread and terror.

Many people misunderstand the purpose of the presentation. They believe that it is designed to be a test of your intellect. This is the cause of much wasted preparation time and usually results in a dull, tedious ramble.

Actually the presentation is a test of your ability to communicate and persuade. This is true even if the panel itself innocently believes that it is about the excellence of your thinking. This does not mean that you can get away with sloppy thinking, only that it is not the prime quality on which the panel judges you. Ability to influence is virtually always on the list of job competencies. This is because it is an essential part of any job. The more senior the job, the more it is likely to be about being able to influence people over whom you have no control. It's about feelings and emotion not about rational thinking. It's also about selling. If you doubt this, think about any time you have faced the task of having to convince people that your opinion or suggested solution to any problem is the correct one. Invariably some element of selling is involved. By this I don't mean selling in its negative sense of overpowering people too foolish or gullible to be able to resist your pressure. In an organization setting, selling is about persuading people that one idea is superior

125

to another. This will often involve a presentation, perhaps just to staff clustered informally around your desk in an office or during a formal meeting in a board room.

Here are some examples

> Dawn wants to improve the layout of the open plan office in which she works. Several of her colleagues like it the way it is, so she will face resistance.
>
> Prash wants to challenge his boss about the way she handles complaints from customers. She's asked him to make a proposal at their next one-to-one meeting.
>
> Kate has to sell an idea to her team about new ways of working; she feels they work competitively. She would like them to be more collaborative.
>
> Angie finds her sales targets too tough and wants to persuade her boss to reduce them.
>
> Mikhal wants the senior team in his organization to endorse a new project. He has been offered a ten-minute slot at the next team meeting to put forward his ideas.

The ability to influence others is possibly the most important single skill you need in order to be successful at work, no matter how senior or junior the job. That is why a sensible employer wants to see how you set about it, and the best way to test whether your claims to be a brilliant influencer match up with reality is to experience you in action. The questions the panel is asking itself are:

Am I convinced by this person? How self-confident is he or she?

Do I like him or her?

If this person were giving a talk to staff, how would they respond?

Am I enjoying listening and watching?

Can I follow the thread of what this person is saying?

Being authentic

The best way to deliver any presentation is to be your authentic self. The secret of achieving authenticity and relaxed authority is first to imagine that you are speaking naturally to people you really care about. You must want to engage them. You must also want to share your own excitement and interest in what you are saying and this means being super-alert to their moment-by-moment responses. Let real emotion come into it: if you feel passionate, show it in how you speak.

The content

It would be rare for selectors to spring the subject of the presentation on to you. Ninety-nine percent of the time you will be informed at least a few days in advance. Organizations show a distinct lack of imagination here. In my experience the topic is most usually a variant of one of these

What would you expect to achieve in your first six months in the job?

What are the challenges facing this team and how would you deal with them?

In effect these are the same topic. You cannot talk about either without having researched what the job and the organization needs. So the presentation is one place where you get the perfect opportunity to demonstrate the quality of your research.

The temptation with either topic is to believe that you should batter the panel into submission by doing a mini-McKinsey analysis of their problems, replete with mind-blowing statistics and very long words. This is a terrible idea. First, you are still an observer and however excellent your research, even when you have managed to get some privileged insider information, you will have limited access to what is actually going on in the organization. Secondly, despite the fact that all organizations believe they are unique the problems that beset most of them are extremely similar: staff who are not motivated, predatory activity from competitors, spiralling

127

costs, lack of innovation, climates of fear and suspicion, poor leadership – and so on. The chances that you will say something startlingly insightful are small. The other danger is that organizational problems are multi-layered. Once you start really trying to analyse all the problems, there is a severe risk that you will get carried away and over-run your allotted time. Beware: if you do this it simply reduces the amount of time that the panel has left for your interview and will leave the impression that you are too fond of your own voice.

Alternative topics

If you are being recruited for a specialist rather than a managerial role, you might be given a variant of one of the above topics. For instance, here are some examples from my own clients:

Project manager	*Outline what the most common human problems are with any project*
Customer complaints manager (an internal appointment and possible promotion)	*Analyse what the common problems of customer care are and how you would solve them*
Management trainer	*Tell us what your favourite management theory is and why*
Sales executive	*Tell us how you see our Brand and what you might suggest to improve it*
Junior buyer, retail chain	*How would you improve relationships with our suppliers?*

Structuring the material

Some ways of organizing your material could include having sections dealing with

Internal factors and external factors

Short-, medium- and long-term priorities

Taking an historical or chronological approach

Analysing what different opinion formers might need – so-called 'stakeholders': these would include staff, customers/clients/regulators/shareholders

Why facts alone don't persuade

Facts, especially statistical ones, have low power to persuade – and remember that this is the purpose of the presentation. This may come as a shock to you, but research has repeatedly shown it to be true. If you ask members of an audience several days or weeks later what the statistics shown in a presentation actually were, their recall will be hazy. People who make their living as 'motivational speakers' addressing large audiences every week, rarely use a single fact in what they say. Their energy goes into creating rapport and emotional connection with the listeners, conveying the feeling that they have a personal message for everyone present. If you have ever heard one of these speakers, ask yourself what you recall. The chances are that you will remember the warm glow, the excitement, the humour – in other words *how* the presentation was given rather than anything specific it contained. The overall reason is that the human brain responds to emotion first and to reasoning second. The limbic system of the brain, the emotional centre, is far more influential than the pre-frontal cortex – the part that deals with judgement and logic.

The way to give a successful presentation is to

- Start positively, never, ever, with something self-deprecatory or apologetic, or with telling the audience that you are nervous. This is often a temptation for women as we may be inclined to believe that this will make the audience be nice to us, whereas it has the opposite effect.
- Constantly weave in what you have gleaned from your research but be personal: talk about your own values and give a flavour of what you would bring to the job.

129

- Paint verbal pictures of what success would look, sound and feel like if all the problems were solved; tell stories (see page 177).
- Concentrate on the human factors.
- Speak without notes.
- Keep your vocabulary simple.
- Keep in constant eye contact with your audience, sweeping them from left to right and then back again.
- Smile.
- Keep to one main point for every three minutes of your presentation, so in a ten-minute presentation you can make three. This is as much as people can remember from a verbal presentation.
- Don't bother with telling people the structure – e.g. 'I have three points'. Forget the 'first tell them what you're going to tell them, then tell them, then tell them what you've told them' principle; it may be useful in an hour-long lecture, though personally I find it a bit tired, but it just gets in the way in a ten-minute piece. Go straight into your first story instead.

The job I was going for represented a big promotion for me and I had the usual subject for the presentation: Describe what you would set out to achieve in your first year in the job and how you would do it. I knew all the problems inside out, but I decided I would adopt the story format. I plunged straight into it, starting

'I want you to imagine that it's <I gave the date – a year from the date of the interview>. You're at a staff meeting. There's a buzz in the room because we're about to present the award for Customer Champion of the Year.'

And then I spun my picture of what would be happening and what had preceded it. I told three other stories. My underpinning framework was that the department's problems all stemmed from complacency about our customers and an unacceptably poor standard of delivery. My stories in effect described changing this through changing the management style of the department, getting the support of the senior people in the company, exposing all the staff to customer focus groups, then training people all over again. I really enjoyed doing the presentation and I could see it was going down well because they were all smiling. Even though I was the outsider candidate, the most junior and the only woman, I got the job and I was told afterwards that my presentation was the clincher. Everyone else did the usual old slides whereas I spoke with a single card of notes and from the heart.

Giving the presentation

It is difficult to learn how to give a presentation from a book, so although I describe here how to do it well, there is actually no substitute for live practice in front of a helpful friend. Time how long it takes – you will be surprised by how easily you use up your allotted time, so plan what to cut at this, the rehearsal stage. Instruct the friend to be ultra-frank and to tell you exactly how you are coming across. Ask for immediate responses: what works? What could be better? What suggestions do they have for improvement? As an additional aid, get the friend to video you with a mobile. Review it together and face up to whatever it reveals.

How to manage your voice

Vocal attractiveness is as much a matter of genes as of training. If you are lucky enough to have a deep, pleasant and sonorous voice which you can project effortlessly, be thankful because you already have an advantage over people with quiet voices or, even worse, voices that are both quiet and squeaky. Women with tiny, high, girlish voices are at a particular disadvantage. A voice that is inaudible, adenoidal, whining or that grates harshly may cause instant rejection. Accent is another difficulty. Social prejudice deems certain British regional accents to be unpleasing, and if you are not a native English speaker, your accent may also be getting in the way for you. Once you have reached adulthood, you can learn, with professional help and a great deal of effort, to modify an accent but it is difficult to make wholesale changes.

Audibility

There is a lot you can do to help yourself. If audibility is your problem you will already know: people at meetings will be leaning forward irritably to hear you, may constantly be asking you to speak up or may miss your entry into the conversation because your voice is so quiet. This is largely a psychological problem made worse by poor breathing habits and can definitely be radically improved. Start with the psychology: you will have learnt at some point in your life that what you had to say didn't matter, or else that nice people don't raise their voices. Often, people with this problem have grown up in tense households where at the same time expressing anger was avoided and punished. If this has been your experience you need to override it by telling yourself that what may have seemed sensible in childhood is not necessarily helpful now. You have the right to be heard.

Learning to project

In a large quiet, empty room, find yourself something to read aloud, ideally a poem or fine piece of rhetoric, but failing that, any old newspaper opinion column will do. Read out a paragraph, keeping one hand just below your collar bone. People with quiet voices are normally 'speaking from the head' so you will feel no vibration. There are five cavities in the body that can be used for resonating: the nose, mouth, throat, voice box and chest, in increasing order of importance. When your voice is inaudible, the chances are you are only using the cavities in your head, straining your throat in the effort to increase volume and not using the chest at all. To project your voice you have to learn to speak from your diaphragm: the powerful muscle that supports the lungs and that is attached to the sternum and spine. When you do 7/11 breathing (see page 65) you will be using your diaphragm. Practise this now and get to remind yourself of how it feels.

Now it's all about intention. Tell yourself that you absolutely do want to communicate with the back wall of the room. Raise your head without tilting it backwards. Put one hand just above your waist and read out your first sentence, noticing the vibration you should now be feeling. Could they hear at the back? Remind yourself: you want them to! It's the determination to reach them that will do it, not straining or shouting. Imagine your voice curving purposefully through the air and landing on that wall. This will feel uncomfortable if you are going against a lifetime's injunctions about being invisible, but keep going. The parts of words that make real noise are the vowels: pay attention to them.

People with tiny voices are often speaking through partially closed mouths. Look at opera singers to see why it matters to open the whole of your mouth. Practise making large, slow mouth movements when speaking and see how it makes an instant difference to your voice power. Be alert too, to any vocal tics you have such as giving little fake coughs before you answer a difficult question, or doing noisy throat-clearing.

> When I asked this candidate why she had left her last job, she evaded my eyes, paused and gave a theatrically loud throat-clear, touched her mouth, apologized for the throat clearing saying she had a cold, and then gave her answer. It was 100% unconvincing and told me she was lying. I was so certain of this I didn't even bother to check with her former employer.

Mobilizing your face and voice

Actors find warm-up exercises useful before going on stage. These can be helpful to you too if you can find a private space to do them before going into the interview room or place where you will be giving a presentation. Your face will be on show and you need to make full use of your facial muscles.

Chewing sticky toffee

Imagine that you have a mouth full of sticky toffee. Chew it vigorously. This gets the muscles of your mouth warmed up. Do this for about a minute.

Sticking your tongue out

Stick your tongue in and out quickly for about a minute. Feeling literally tongue tied is a common handicap. This exercise gets you round it.

Massaging your face

Work around your face with both hands, massaging gently. This helps the whole face to feel warmed up.

Try a few tongue twisters to get your voice going:

> *Round and round the rugged rock the ragged rascal ran*
>
> *Two toads totally tired trying to trot to Tetbury*
>
> *She sells sea shells on the sea shore*
>
> *Three grey geese on the green grass grazing*
>
> *She is a thistle-sifter and she has a sieve of sifted thistles and a sieve of unsifted thistles*

Speed and articulation

Certain commonplace *elisions* – contractions of words and phrases – are not welcome at a job interview because they may suggest, totally unfairly I agree, either that you are under-educated or that your work might have the same sloppy characteristics. If you commonly use any of them, correct yourself now

Word	Translation
Gonna	Going to
Wanna	Want to
Yeah	Yes
Lorra	Lot of
Gorra	Got to
Innit?	Isn't it?

Another unfortunate habit with the same impact is pronouncing -*ing* words as -*ink*, often combined for some Londoners with pronouncing *th* as *ff*, so the word *something* can come out as *some-ffink*. Whatever your accent, it's always possible to improve articulation.

> I come from Kerala and considered my English to be good. It was, in the sense that it was fluent and grammatical. But I was persistently failing to get promotion as a doctor from Senior Registrar to consultant. It was only when a kind boss recommended coaching that I realized how difficult it was to understand me. My coach told me I was speaking at twice the 'normal' speed in the UK, that my articulation was poor and my strong accent meant that people just couldn't make out what I was saying: in fact she couldn't!

When I worked with this client I asked her to read aloud one of Roald Dahl's Revolting Rhymes (excellent for practice as they are funny and can also be declaimed and read in different ways for differing effect). She was speaking at a racing commentator rate – 375 words a minute. She was astonished to learn that newsreader speed is 110–120 words a minute. Learning to slow right down made instant improvements in her ability to communicate. To do the same, calculate the number of words in the passage you are going to read aloud. Set a stopwatch and read aloud at your normal speed. Now see if you can slow it, pausing for emphasis and effect and also varying your speed. If it's too slow, your listeners will get restless. If it's too fast they will switch off. Ideally you should aim for 150–160 words per minute. If you are finding this hard, read it again, this time concentrating on speaking any three syllable words by giving them their actual three syllables, holding the emphasis on the vowel sounds.

A hesitant speaker is often one who swallows consonants at the ends of words. If this is your problem, tongue twisters can help (see page 134).

It is worth tackling this problem as it will be getting in the way for you in everyday life as well as in the context of selection for a job. To make lasting improvements you need to practise for at least 15 minutes every single day and devote real effort to it. If you leave it until the day before the interview or presentation, that will be too late.

Using your body

Stand up – or not? If you can, always stand. It gives you more authority and this is harder to achieve if you are sitting down. But you must judge this at the time. For instance, if the interview room is small and everyone is hunched around a minute table, standing will not be appropriate. Stand with your body upright but not rigid facing your audience straight on. Mentally stake out your space and use it to take a few steps backwards and forwards at key moments while you are speaking. If you remain rooted to the spot you will convey 'tethered elephant' and if you pace about too much, 'caged lion' – neither is desirable.

Watch out for any of these mannerisms, as they may all convey lack of authority:

Mannerism	Effect on audience
Leaning on one foot	Reduces your height and therefore your authority
Crossing one leg over the other	As above, but looks as if you actually want to seem smaller
Cocking your head on one side	A particular problem with women, conveying, 'please like me'
Turning away from your audience/ shoulder pointing to the door	Suggests 'Get me out of here!'
Hunching your shoulders	Suggests nervousness and tension
'Steepling' your hands	Looks pompous

Other common mannerisms include: nervous little coughs, jingling change in your pocket, scratching, pushing glasses up your nose, pushing sleeves up, doing a 'fig-leaf' – putting hands over your genital area. If you find you are indulging in any of these, practise until you have eliminated them.

Check that everyone can hear you before you get going properly. Pause for two or three seconds before starting your presentation – this gives a little added drama and allows you to get your thoughts together – and use pauses for added impact while you are speaking.

Use the *lighthouse effect* – this means raking your audience slowly from one side to the other throughout your presentation, engaging everyone in a few seconds of regular eye contact. This retains their interest and creates the impression that you are talking to each person individually. It also gives you immediate feedback – who is looking bored? asleep? fidgety? Beware of talking to only one side of the room, to the ceiling, to your notes, your screen, your feet, the spaces above or between the chairs.

The role of PowerPoint

Essentially: don't use it. You will be transfixed by the technology and by worries about whether or not it will work; you could end up repeating the words on the screen, just in case your audience has missed some of them. Your audience will be looking at the screen not at you. You may be looking at the laptop screen or even worse, turning to read the projected image behind you and away from the audience. When you do all this, you will not be in eye contact and therefore you will not be in rapport. Increasingly I find clients telling me that they have specifically been told not to use PowerPoint, for all the reasons above. If you feel you need notes, use a simple system of blank index cards with a few key words on them. Punch a hole in the top right corner and hold the cards together with a treasury tag so that they cannot get out of order.

What if the panel has commanded PowerPoint?

You may encounter this, or alternatively you may feel nervous without the back up reminder that PowerPoint provides. If so, my advice is to limit your slides to two per three minutes, so in a ten-minute presentation you should have no more than six, including your introductory slide. Each slide should have a limit of 30 words and 200 characters including spaces and be in a large typeface.

Vocabulary

The English language is extraordinary in that it draws on two main sources of vocabulary: French and Anglo-Saxon. When the Normans invaded in the 11th century, Anglo Saxon, of Germanic origin, remained the language of the general population. Meanwhile French, which is derived from Latin, became the official language – of government, the court and the judicial system. Words of French origin still dominate here: long words of three or more syllables ending for instance in -tion, -ize, -ment, -ive. When Modern English eventually emerged in the early 16th century, it drew on both languages. When people want to seem impressive and official, they tend to use French-origin words, even though these are harder to read and understand than the more direct, shorter words of Anglo-Saxon origin. So someone might say *commence* when they mean start, or *necessitate* when they mean need, or *obligated* when they

138

mean bound. If you absolutely have to use PowerPoint, write as much of it in Anglo-Saxon as you can.

Here is an example, drawn with his permission straight from the proposed presentation of one client I was coaching for a senior executive job. He was asked to describe how he would improve the bottom line results of his department – in other words just another variant of the standard presentation topic. This was his first attempt at one slide

Reducing expenditure

- Facilitate immediate empowerment of staff through culture change programme
- Incentivize staff suggestions that are implemented
- Employ alternative contracting agencies
- Ameliorate excessive use of landline telephones through discouraging utilization
- Determine optimal methodologies for disseminating expenditure-reduction programmes to staff

This horrible piece of verbiage, clotted with even more horrible management jargon, was destined to cause him severe problems at the presentation. When I pointed this out his pained reply was, 'Well this is how they talk to each other'. I had to tell him that I doubted it. When people are really communicating do they use words like *optimize* or *ameliorate*? There are 44 words on this slide and 360 characters, including spaces.

Together we rewrote it like this

Cutting costs

- Encourage staff to offer ideas
- Reward staff whose ideas are taken up
- Change to cheaper suppliers
- Cut staff use of landlines
- Find ways of selling this to staff

139

There are 35 words here and only 151 characters. It is much easier to read and the meaning is far clearer.

You may be asked to prepare and bring a copy of your notes. If so, and even if not, back up your presentation with a simple one page handout, written again in simple English. This should not be merely a reproduction of your slides but specially composed to be read in paragraphs, like a normal piece of prose, maybe with a few bullet points. If you print out those PowerPoint slides from the Notes menu you will probably be handing the panel more than one piece of paper. This makes it most unlikely that your handout will be read.

Ending

I have seen many people give good presentations and then spoil the effect by letting their voices trail away apologetically at the end. You need a proper ending, ideally one that links with your opening sentence. Don't smirk, rub your hands across your face or do any 'phew that was awful, glad that's over' facial grimacing as it will instantly undermine the power of what you have been saying.

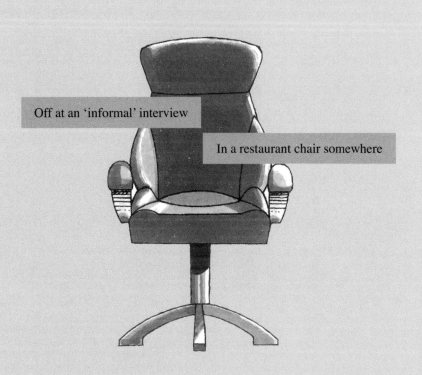

Off at an 'informal' interview

In a restaurant chair somewhere

9 SOCIAL EVENTS

> **Myth**: informal social events are not that important
>
> **Reality**: they matter

A senior manager of my acquaintance once claimed that you can tell everything you need to know about a candidate from how they behave with you in a restaurant and suggested that interviews were therefore unnecessary. All you needed to do was to invite the person to eat with you. A person who treats the waiter rudely? Would be the same with junior colleagues. Can't ask you a single question about yourself? No people skills. Someone who says she's not fussy and will eat everything except rice, fish, mushrooms, red meat, spinach, celery, onions . . . this is the person who will be off sick with every minor ailment. Orders the most expensive item on the menu? Will want a high-end Mac when everyone else makes do with Microsoft. Drinks too much wine and blabs indiscreetly about current colleagues? Could never be trusted not to do the same in a new job.

This man was only half serious but essentially he was right in his underlying assumptions: that we give a lot away about ourselves in social situations, often more than we realize. This is why it is increasingly common for employers to build in a variety of social events to the selection process. You may be asked to

Meet over drinks with other candidates and the panel

Join an informal group of staff over lunch in their restaurant

Take part in a social event where members of staff are present along with important external contacts

Have lunch or dinner with your potential future boss: usually only for the most senior jobs

These occasions are a good idea because they allow selectors to see how you handle yourself in a social setting. This does matter in a surprisingly large number of jobs. From your point of view such events are also helpful as they give you further opportunities to find out about what the organization looks like from the inside

145

and, while your potential future bosses are looking at you, you can be looking at them.

How should you behave?

Accept first that you are being assessed every moment you are with the potential employer and their staff. Even if more junior or peripheral staff do not have a formal vote in the process, their opinions will be canvassed. Your aim throughout is to do two things. One is to gather more information about the organization and the job. Remember that if what you discover creates unease and it emerges that the job is a poor fit for you (see chapter 1) it is still possible to withdraw before the final selection stages. The second purpose is to give people a more rounded idea of who you are and what it would be like working with you.

What is being assessed?

- How much you are at ease with yourself
- How you cope with what is potentially a stressful situation disguised as a social gathering
- How courteous, open, friendly and co-operative you are
- How much genuine interest you show in other people
- How likeable you seem
- How well you would represent your team or the organization in gatherings of influential external or senior staff contacts

Few of us are all of these things all of the time, but the idea, as at every stage of the selection process, is to show selectors your best possible self.

These social events are often referred to as 'Trial by Orange Juice'. The idea of being on trial is not helpful (see page 61) but the phrase does convey the terror many people feel about being alone in a roomful of strangers.

146

Fear of rejection

All of the negative self-talk that we do when faced with people we don't know has its roots in fear of rejection: the ultimate punishment for herd animals. However, our excuses don't stand up to any real scrutiny:

The excuse	The reality
I learnt never to talk to strangers.	They're not strangers: they have something in common with you, that's why you're all there
You can't talk to someone if you haven't been introduced	You don't need to wait for someone to introduce you – you can introduce yourself
I've got nothing to say to people I don't know	How do you know they've got nothing to say to *you*?
You shouldn't be pushy – who'd want to talk to me? All these people are more important and interesting	Risk is the name of the game – you'll never know the truth unless you make the effort
I can't make small talk	It's a way of putting others at ease so everyone needs to learn how to do it

Events to meet staff or stakeholders

This is usually a stand-up event, a version of a drinks and canapés party. First, investigate the guest list. Who will be there? What background research might you do to find out something about them in advance? Ask for this information from whoever is organizing the event and google the names. Secondly, see yourself as an active guest who can help the host make the event go well: this is the major transformation in attitude that you need to make. A needy guest waits patiently to be introduced, hangs back, wants to be looked after. An active guest does the opposite: takes the initiative, introduces himself or herself, introduces people to each other, ferries food and drink. This rule applies even when you yourself are under scrutiny. As an active guest, you are concerned with others,

147

not with yourself. The secret of defeating social shyness is to lose the preoccupation with yourself. So for instance, if you are sitting around a table and no one else seems inclined to take the lead here, take on the host role: introduce yourself and ask everyone round the table to do the same.

Be ready to introduce yourself to people and prepare a one sentence introduction. This should go beyond your name and job description. Examples might be

Police Officer

I'm Chris Jones and I'm one of the people responsible for keeping (name of County's) streets safe

Senior Nurse

I'm Chris Jones and I run the general surgery ward at <name of hospital>

Facilities manager

I'm Chris Jones, the Bricks and Boilers person for <name of organization>

Repeat people's names when you are introduced – that way you are more likely to remember them. Ask again if you've forgotten. Say your own name, even if you think the other person should already know yours. Similarly, if someone greets you and you can't remember their name, ask. Apologize, saying something like

I'm hopeless at names – I'm afraid I've forgotten yours . . .

Working the room

First you should mentally divide the room into four and plan to work your way around each quadrant in turn. Look for trios rather than pairs to approach. Pairs may be having an intense conversation and are more difficult to break into. Trios are unlikely to be so preoccupied. Attach yourself to the trio. Join in at first with nods, eye contact and other attentive body language. Wait for a brief pause in the conversation, then introduce yourself and

148

make some contribution to the discussion, depending on what you have just heard. If you have a name badge, wear it on the right as this is easier for people to read without peering or breaking eye contact.

Offer your hand to everyone (see page 94).

Small talk

Small talk is one of the ways we get to feel safe and accepted by others. *Your main aim: find out what you have in common with the other person.* Useful tactics:

Journeys to the venue and comments about the weather

Everyone understands that this is a ritual exchange and that neither party is really interested in the answers. Beware of appearing to moan too much – for instance about the evils of London Transport or about the terminal grimness of the weather. Never tell travel stories about only just making it on time, even if any delays were not your fault as, regardless of what you say, drawing attention to the delays might imply that you would be an habitual late-arriver if you got the job.

Observation: on the event. This should not be critical, as in 'what a terrible venue, this hotel could do with a customer care programme . . .' Bland is safer:

This is a beautiful room. There are more people here than I expected.

Offer: something about yourself that's relevant to the event:

I'm here as a candidate, of course, but currently I work at . . .

Enquire: into the other person's interest in the event:

What brings you here?
What's your role in the organization?

Enquire about their job. Virtually everyone can talk at length about their work. Use open questions which encourage talking. Good questions here could be:

What does your job actually involve?
So what do you do in a typical day?

Ideally you are looking to establish something in common with everyone you meet. So you might add a few other clues about your interests as you answer questions or give people information which will entice them into revealing a parallel interest. This is a real example, given to me by a client:

Candidate: Yes, my journey here was fine, thanks. I live in Didsbury so I decided to walk here. I'm on a keeping-fitter regime and I've given myself the target of a five mile walk every day so this was a good way of getting that in.

Other guest: I do that too and I use a pedometer – do you have one?

Candidate: yes I do and <then you talk about walking and fitness, or which make of pedometer is best>

Candidate: My current job is with <Name of Council> Social services. I'm one of the child protection team so as you can imagine I'm very interested in the current story about <name of any current or recent child protection scandal in a different authority>

Other guest: Oh, I've always thought that must be a very tricky job to do well; intervene too much and you're in trouble, intervene too little and the press is after you.

Candidate: That's so true <then conversation takes off on a topic of mutual interest>

When you meet someone who can help you understand the organization and the job, ask similar questions to the ones you will have already asked at the earlier stage of research. Never seem to be tempting the other person into a gossipy indiscretion, for instance into probing the possibly unflattering reasons why a predecessor left. Keep your questions neutral, e.g.

What do you think are the main challenges that the successful candidate will face?

When you meet the other candidates you should behave in exactly the same way as with everyone else present. They may be prickly, guarded and hostile. Alternatively they may be haughty and patronizing or gushing and self-deprecating. If so, this is foolish. Do your best to help them relax or unbend, and if you get nowhere just wish them luck and move on. Sometimes there is a temptation for all the candidates to huddle together for mutual protection: not a good idea as it will convey social awkwardness and in any case the whole purpose of the event is to meet the staff.

As ever it's important to manage your body language throughout (chapter 6). You are aiming for comfortable self confidence. Stand straight and square on to the other person (no slouching, no crossed arms, no pointing your shoulder at them or jigging on one hip). Keep eye contact but beware of staring. Smile, be enthusiastic, be pleased to be talking to them.

Moving around

Don't overstay your welcome with any one group or individual – the point of the event is to mingle with as many people as possible. Move away when you've finished something you're saying rather than after the other person has been speaking. Offer your hand again and say something like, 'It's been really pleasant to meet you' then leave cleanly. Move at least a quarter of the room away. Alternative tactics could include

Saying, 'I'm ready for some food/another drink – are you?' If your offer of a fresh drink is accepted, bring it and then move off straight away, using one of the lines of dialogue below.

Saying, 'I need to find <the loo; person X; the event organizer>; and say goodbye as above.

151

Take the person with you to meet someone else, then leave them chatting with the new person.

Beware of over-selling

These social events are not interviews in disguise. Their purpose is entirely to assess your social skills and to give you a little low-key exposure to some of the people who might be future colleagues. They are not occasions for mini-speeches about your strategy if appointed, or for unrestrained bragging about your skills. Nor is it appropriate to indulge in undue modesty. People already on the staff may well ask you about your current job and probe you a little about your application. Answer simply and straightforwardly but keep it brief, then turn your interest to them so that the whole thing more nearly resembles a normal social conversation.

Restaurant events

If you have got as far as receiving a solo dining invitation you are close to landing the job. Euphoria or feeling flattered can mean danger that you sabotage yourself at this stage through unguarded behaviour. You are still being assessed so everything earlier in this chapter still applies, including allowing yourself the freedom to withdraw if what you experience is off-putting. Normally this event will be with your potential boss. Sometimes it will be a threesome: the boss and his or her boss as well and this can be more difficult to manage. A trio is always an awkward number often ending up with two against one so you need to do what you can to avoid feeling either excluded or getting over-cosy with one of the other two. Remember that the hirers can also reveal more about themselves than they intend.

> The boss told me he was inviting his boss to meet me as well. After they had both drunk quite a lot it became clear that the boss was totally in awe of the more senior man who became more and more pompous and didactic as the evening went

152

on. This man began a conversation with me and more or less excluded the other guy. It was a fair warning about what awaited me. I was offered and did accept the job, and I was glad I'd had the chance to consider all of this before I started as this relationship was critical to making the department work, but I did consider withdrawing at this stage.

The rules here are to be cautiously friendly and to establish the purported aims of the event in advance. Some possible answers are: explore what kind of package you would want; discuss in more detail your approach to the job (in this case you may be down to being one of the last two candidates) or further aspects of your bid already raised in an interview. It helps to put a time limit on the meal – for instance offering a plausible reason for your need to be away by a particular time: two hours is usually quite long enough.

Ordering food

Take your cue from your host. If he or she does not order a starter, don't have one yourself. Pick a menu item in the same price range. In an expensive restaurant, leave the waiter to drape your napkin on your lap and to pour wine and water. Where alcohol is concerned it is now unusual to order wine for lunch, even a single glass, and perfectly all right to refuse it on the grounds that it will make you sleepy in the afternoon. You may also be wise to refuse alcohol with dinner because alcohol has an immediately disinhibiting effect, but beware of seeming either puritanical or of raising the possibility that you have a drinking problem. Some of my clients have told the white lie that they are taking a particular antibiotic (flagyl or metronidazole for example where it is dangerous to mix the drug with alcohol). In general, only have alcohol if the host is having it. Even if the host shows every intention of getting drunk, restrict yourself to one glass. Never order food that is difficult or messy to eat, so beware spaghetti, steaks, soups full of

153

trailing bits, fish that you have to fillet for yourself, lobster and other seafood served in its shell, asparagus, an unpeeled orange.

When faced with a battery of cutlery, start from the outside and work in. Grasp the knife by wrapping your whole hand around it. Don't hold it like a pen – I know this is trivial and entirely about social snobbery, but this is a middle class cultural norm and I know of one boss who was tempted to reject the favoured candidate at this stage on the grounds that 'he held his knife like a working class oik'. If your mother never cured you of peculiar ways of using your cutlery, now is the time to cure yourself. You want to look socially sophisticated, not a childish freak who, for instance can only eat with a spoon, or by holding your cutlery the 'wrong' way around. Don't wolf down bread rolls while you are waiting for the first course. Start eating when your host starts and eat at the same pace. Don't talk while eating; don't eat with your mouth open or lean with your elbows on the table or sticking out at an angle and do use the napkin to blot your mouth from time to time so that there are no stray splodges of food to distract your companion.

Write a brief, warm email or handwritten note after the event saying how much you enjoyed the food, the choice of restaurant and the company of your host. Reaffirm your interest in the job and say you look forward to the next steps.

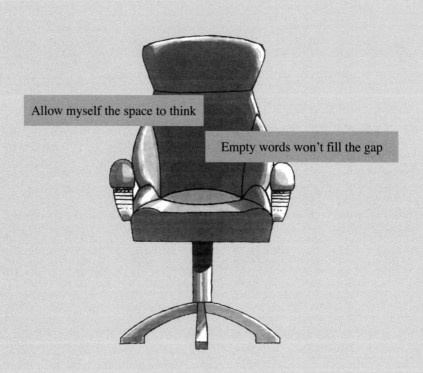

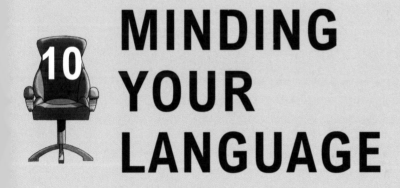

10 MINDING YOUR LANGUAGE

> **f f** **Myth**: You can't help how you speak
>
> **Reality**: Self awareness about the words you use can make a huge and positive difference **, ,**

When I work with clients on honing their interview skills, I listen closely to the words they are using. I find that many people are oblivious to how they can spoil their chances of getting the job through the language they use, largely because they are unaware of their own speech patterns. Make sure this doesn't happen to you.

Use direct, clear language

Indirect and fuzzy language can be a problem and there are three ways it can blur the message you want to deliver.

Garlanding your words with 'modifiers'

This may be a particular trap for British people. Our preoccupation with seeming modest, or with wanting to avoid appearing over-emphatic because that might be like conveying that we think our opinions matter more than someone else's, means that we constantly use words like these: *a bit*; *quite*; *rather*; *almost*; *pretty*; *not bad at* . . . Often our true meaning is the opposite. So when someone British says, I'm really quite interested in buying your house, what they probably mean is 'I'm mad keen to buy your house'. And 'I'm a bit of a fan of Italian food' actually means 'I love it!'

While these may serve our purposes in ordinary conversation, they are totally misplaced in a job interview.

Compare this

> *I'm pretty skilled at using Excel*

with

> *I've used Excel for 8 years and I know how to make it do anything I want!*

159

The underlying meaning is the same. In the first statement, the speaker means 'Yes! I'm an expert at spreadsheets' but leaves listeners to work out for themselves whether it means they are a modest beginner or an authority. In the second, the meaning is unmistakeable. If you have skill or consider yourself good at something, then say it cleanly.

Phrases that convey uncertainty

Years ago I was having a conversation with my then boss about meeting an important deadline imposed by his boss. In attempting to reassure him that my team would do what was required, I used the phrase 'We'll try our best'. As his anxiety levels rose and he kept asking me again whether or not we would meet this target, so did my exasperation. 'Yes, of course, we'll try our very best', wondering why this was not enough to make him drop the subject. Of course I now see that using a phrase like 'try' conveyed the possibility of failure or lack of commitment, whereas actually I was certain that we would be successful. What I should have said was 'Yes, we can do it – it will take effort but it's a priority and we'll hit that target'.

Beware of falling into the same trap in a job interview.

> *'How do you think you'll cope with working on Saturdays?'*

> *'I'll do my best not to let you down.'*

Effect conveyed to potential future boss: you could let her down.

Other phrases to avoid include: *I hope I can*; *I'm not really sure*; *I don't know*; *maybe I could*; *it would be a bit of a stretch*; *possibly*; *I could give it a try I suppose* . . .

Verbal fillers

The other way we sabotage ourselves is by being unaware of how often we use verbal fillers. These are so common that we may fail to notice them in others, let alone in ourselves.

160

Well, I think it's **sort of** obvious isn't it, **you know**, that the trends in the retail market are for, **I mean**, the value end to be making more money because in a recession, **kind of** it's clear, **err**, that people, **you know, umm**, are **actually** more wary of spending their money so **basically** it's the way the market is going, **do you see what I'm saying**?

You may think the above is an exaggeration but it's not that far off how many of us speak when we are still working out what to say. In a job interview it will be noticed and will convey lack of articulacy or else chronic uncertainty about your own opinions. Once people notice the pattern they may start counting how often you commit the offence and this means that they will not be listening to the content of what you are saying. The solution is first to assess how far you do it and then to get rid of it from your everyday speech. Another tactic is to prepare confidently so that when you do speak you are able to talk without fillers. Fillers provide us with thinking space and the best solution is to provide it for ourselves with – silence. Just pause. Don't fill the gap with anything.

Crude boasting

The TV programme *The Apprentice* probably has a lot to answer for here. The majority of the naïve young people who appear on the programme seem to have got it into their heads that the way to impress Alan Sugar, lordly before he was actually made a lord, is to tell him repeatedly how brilliant they are. 'Hire me,' they beg, 'I'm the best salesman you'll ever meet.' This is often followed by spiteful attempts to blame their colleagues for anything that has gone wrong in their joint tasks. Of course the shameful joy of the programme is the swiftly offered evidence that they are not at all brilliant.

While it is legitimate to describe the detailed evidence of your successes it looks absurd to make flowery and grandiose claims, especially claims that you are better than anyone else. These are empty promises and as with the hapless competitors in

The Apprentice, they immediately reveal a comical lack of self-awareness.

> *I'll give it 150%*
>
> *I beat everyone else in meeting my targets*
>
> *I'm brilliant at . . .*
>
> *I'd like to be doing your job by next year*
>
> *I could help you do your job even better*
>
> *If you offer me a job you won't regret it*
>
> *I'm easily the most outstanding candidate*

Careless language

Never forget that the interview is a social exchange. I have often seen candidates unintentionally annoy interviewers by careless use of language. What happens is this: the candidate is dismayed or startled by something the interviewer has asked. The candidate wants to disagree or ask a clarifying question but doesn't know how to do it.

Interviewer	*What's your experience of x?*
Candidate	*Why are you asking that?*
Effect on interviewer	The word 'why?' comes across as rude because it implies that the question is out of line and, in effect, orders the interviewer to justify asking it.

Don't ever start a sentence with the word *why*. If your real request is for further clarification then say, 'Could you tell me a bit more about what you need to know here?'

Interviewer	*This company is facing a decline in our revenue from x. I wonder what ideas you might have about how to get us back on track?*
Candidate	*With respect, I think I'd like to change that question to something else . . .* Alternatives, both equally unwise: *I'm not being funny here, BUT* or *I don't mean to be rude, BUT*
Effect on interviewer	The phrase 'with respect' and others like it always means 'without respect – that was a really stupid question'. 'I don't mean to be rude' tells the interviewer that rude is exactly what you do mean to be.

Never use the phrase 'with respect'. Answer the question in the terms in which it is asked.

Interviewer	*How do you typically handle the problem of Y?*
Candidate	*To be honest, I . . .*
Effect on interviewer	The phrases *to be honest* and *to be frank* alert the interviewer to the probability of a lie or partial truth.

Jargon and clichés

If you are a candidate for a managerial job, do everything you can to avoid using managerial jargon and clichés. They are a substitute for real thinking and have a high potential to irritate. Common ones include:

The strategic envelope, blue sky thinking, throw some spaghetti at the wall and see what sticks, level playing field, moving the goalposts, learning organization, quality time, work-life balance, low-hanging fruit, thinking outside the box, working smarter not harder, let's park that off-line, keeping you in the loop – and hundreds of others.

163

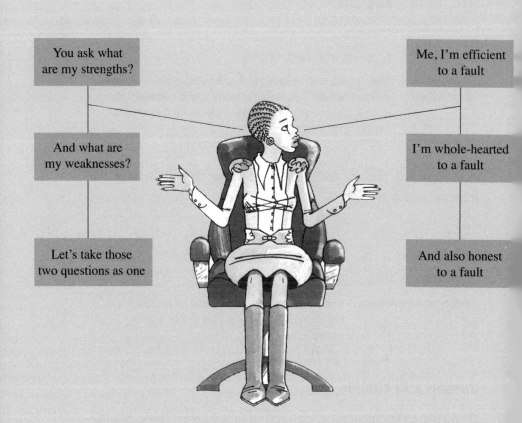

11
ANSWERING THE PREDICTABLE QUESTIONS

> **"** **Myth**: interview questions are a mystery – you can never predict what they are going to ask
>
> **Reality**: most interview questions are entirely predictable **""**

In a well managed organization, the traditional panel interview will probably play a minor part in the hiring process because the emphasis will be on an assessment centre (chapter 7). In companies which have not benefitted from contemporary wisdom on these matters, you may still find the employer relying on an interview as the only way of selecting people. Either way, it is often the part of the whole hiring process that candidates dread – and sometimes interviewers dread it too because the fear of making the wrong choice can be overwhelming.

For all its appearance of rationality and seriousness, choices on both sides of the interviewing table are made on the basis of emotion, later justified on rational grounds. What really sways interviewers are answers to these questions – the ones that are NEVER asked out loud at an interview

Do I like this person?

Are they just like me?

Would I enjoy working with them?

Will they fit in?

Can they reassure me that they have already been successful in doing the kind of work this job needs?

Do they really want this job?

These questions are about likeability, motivation and social skill, some of which is decided on grounds of how you dress, how you handle nervousness and how you sit, stand, use language and talk, all subjects of previous chapters. Where the traditional interview is concerned, the research shows convincingly that the only things it can actually measure are your social skills and motivation. That is why, although the content of your answers is important, *how* you

167

answer in terms of your general behaviour matters every bit as much.

What all employers want

To answer those unasked but vitally important questions, interviewers are on the alert for signs of trouble. Unfortunately, they are looking for ways to exclude rather than include you. This is why you must demonstrate the qualities that all employers want, regardless of level of job, sector or qualifications. Again, these questions are rarely asked openly, but be assured that they are always asked inwardly

Is this person what I want –	Rather than what I don't want –
A problem solver: someone who gets on with things, uses their initiative sensibly?	A problem creator: someone who waits to be told, or takes stupid risks?
Enthusiastic, sunny, optimistic?	A grumbler, complainer, whiner?
A giver: prepared to put other people's interests first?	A taker, looks to further their own interests at the expense of customers, the company or colleagues?
Willing to go the extra mile, to put themselves out, be flexible?	Someone who stands on their dignity, says it's not in their job description, inflexible?
Someone with good people skills?	Someone who annoys others? Creates hostility and conflict?
Puts customers first?	Puts customers down?
Healthy and fit?	Unhealthy and unfit; likely to take a lot of time off?
Committed and determined; persistent in the face of difficulties?	Someone who gives up easily, lacks courage?

Everything you say and do at the interview must therefore be underpinned by the qualities on the left hand side of this table.

Keeping it succinct

Your answers to questions should never be more than three minutes and ideally only two minutes. This is because in a typical 60 minute interview, there will be five minutes spent on getting into and out of the room, on ritual civilities or on trying to catch up on timetable slippage. That leaves 55 minutes. If you have three interviewers, they will probably have allocated themselves three questions each. That makes nine questions. Let's assume that each question takes between 5 and 30 seconds to ask, that leaves just over 50 minutes. That's 5½ minutes for each question: 3 minutes for your answer and 2½ for a follow up question and answer. If you ramble on and on, it will mean that fewer questions can be asked, so you will be at an immediate disadvantage. Also you will be conveying a negative impression: that you are someone unaware of how much you talk, an immediate black mark on the list above, as people who lack self-awareness are also likely to lack people skills. If you don't know how long two minutes is, time yourself with a stop-watch. Two minutes may not seem very long, but bear in mind that TV advertisers pay thousands of pounds for ads that often only last a few seconds and still manage to make an impact.

Being enthusiastic

The employer wants commitment and enthusiasm. It's no good just alleging that you are enthusiastic. You must exude it. This does not mean faking being a bouncy extrovert when actually you are a thoughtful introvert. It does mean that you must smile, sound interested, delighted, pleased to be talking to them and passionate about what you currently do, even if you and your current job have fallen out of love and you know it is time to move on. This is why you must never, ever, criticize your current company, colleagues or boss. The potential employer will immediately think, 'Well if he is saying this about them, he could be saying the same about me in two years' time.' It looks, sounds and is disloyal and no one wants a disloyal staff member.

169

The entirely predictable questions

It's true that of course you can never forecast exactly how a question will be put and you need to listen carefully to the phrasing. But in 90% of interviews, the questions follow a completely foreseeable pattern. You need to note that in every case there is the question that is being asked and the question that is unasked. The question that is unasked is always more important because it is about the doubts that the employer has and on which he or she needs reassurance.

The opening question: normally about your current role

On the surface this is a bland, helpful question intended to settle down a nervous candidate and one that anyone could apparently answer with ease because it's about our favourite specialist subject: ourselves.

Asked question: *What are you currently doing?*

Variants: *Tell us a bit about yourself.* Or, *I see you are currently working as a . . . What does that involve exactly?* Or, *What do you do in a typical day?*

Unasked question: *Does anything you currently do have anything at all to do with what we want?* The yawning trap awaiting you here is to babble on about your life in your current role, or even worse, just your life generally, without making the link to the job on offer.

How to answer

This is where research will pay off. Before the interview, divide a piece of paper in two. On one side, make a list of the skills or tasks that the potential employer wants. On the other side list what you currently do. Pick the three or four areas that are the best match and ignore the others. In answering the question, describe the areas that match well, using similar words to the language the employer has used to describe the job, remembering to keep to the two minute limit.

The why you want the job question

This is probably the most important single question in the interview, although unfortunately, many candidates assume it is the least important. It is usually asked early in the interview, often as the second question.

> They asked me why I wanted the job and I thought it was a totally stupid question. Of course I wanted it! Why else would I be there? I replied on these lines. The HR person told me later that everything I said after that was a waste of time because the boss was so offended by what he saw as my 'rudeness'. I've never made that mistake again.

> I was applying for a job in an accountancy firm that was going through a difficult time. It was less successful than the one I was planning on leaving. Somehow I felt it was an 'inferior' firm. When they asked me the why do you want the job question, I thought I'd given a convincing answer but I didn't get the job and the head-hunter told me the reason was that they thought I believed it to be beneath me because of how I answered. So I lost it only five minutes into the interview!

> When we asked one of the strongest candidates – on paper at least – why she wanted the job she replied that she thought it was our role to sell it to her because she wasn't sure. End of candidate!

President Obama has described being interviewed for a $1m role at a time in 2000 when his private ambition was to build a political career. He tells of his hands shaking with fear that he would be offered the job. I imagine that there was little danger of this as his lack of motivation would have been perfectly obvious, especially in someone whose personal values are so clear.

Asked question: *What attracts you to this job?*

Variants: Why do you want this job? Why would someone like you want to move here?

Unasked questions: *Are you really serious about this? If we offered it to you would you take it? Would you stay – or are you a flitter? Are you applying because you're desperate for any old job?*

Apart from the dangers of appearing luke-warm or rude and abrupt in answering this question, the other major hazard is implying that you want the job because of what it will do for you. Typically self-damaging answers here are talking about how you believe the benefits are superior to anything you currently get; you want a salary increase; you want 'a challenge'; your wife has relocated to Scotland and you want to follow her there and this job is in Scotland so it seems a good fit or it's the next logical step in your career. Sadly, the employer has not the slightest interest in providing you with a career ladder or in solving your domestic and financial problems. Remember that employers are only really concerned with what problems you can solve for them.

How to answer

Ideally your answer has four parts

1. Focused, research-based answers about the attractions for you of the organization, why you admire it, demonstrating your grasp of the essentials that the job needs. The purpose of this part of the answer is to show that you have researched the job and organization properly and that your decision to bid for it is based on facts not fantasy. It is also intended to flatter the employer by showing how much interest you have taken.

2. A summary statement about how you believe your skills and experience are a good fit and how keen you are to bring them to the job. The purpose of this is to start the process of demonstrating how well your skills match what the employer is looking for.

3. A brief mention of your personal values and why you believe in the mission and purpose of the organization and how every previous job you have had has been about these values. This is because true employee commitment happens when people believe that their work has meaning beyond just 'doing a job' – that it does some good for society at large or benefits people in other ways and most employers know this to be true.

4. A final brief conclusion about how it fits your personal circumstances.

Here is how one candidate applied this formula. She was bidding for a job as manager of a niche fashion retail store in London aimed at women aged 18–35. The question she was asked was: *Why would you want this job when you're already working for <a bigger competitor>? Wouldn't you do better to stay put and work your way up with them?*

> I've always liked the clothing you sell because somehow you combine simplicity and interesting cloth with a quirky take on current trends. I wear it a lot myself because I'm bang in your biggest customer segment <she describes some other customer segments, based on her research>. I love the cheeky advertising campaign you currently have on the buses <she describes this> and every time I come into one of the stores I feel a buzz. I've noticed you've recently changed the store layout <she describes it and why it has worked for her> and I admire the way you've been able to keep your prices down through <she describes what her research has shown about their recent supply chain improvements>.

173

I know I'm a natural retailer, I love selling and I love selling to your target age group because I know who they are, in fact I'm one of them! We don't just want something we can get anywhere and I'm confident I know what we – and they – are looking for. I see the difference it can make to a young woman's self confidence to wear great pieces. Also in my current job I've acquired a taste for management. i enjoy the whole thing of motivating a team of people and I'm proud of what I've achieved <she gives a couple of brief examples> and of knowing I've increasing our turnover in my department <she says by how much and over what period of time>.

My hunch is that what you really care about is providing high-quality fashion at affordable prices and that you also care about responsible sourcing, and this matters to me because I want to work for a company that treats suppliers well and of course this makes long-term business sense anyway.

Finally, I'm ready for more responsibility, I'd love the chance to manage an entire store and I'd look forward to bringing you a lot of enthusiasm, energy and commitment for this job.

This candidate was later told that her answer was 'a knock out' and that the entire panel had privately decide to appoint her at this point, only twelve minutes into the interview. Note how well she conveyed detailed knowledge of the company, admiration for its products and values, her personal values, several highly relevant skills, impressive achievement and, of course, totally believable enthusiasm – without in any way putting down her current employer.

The challenges of the job question

Asked question: *What do you see as the main challenges in this job?*

Unasked question: *How realistic are you? How much research have you done?*

This question is a mini-version of the most popular topic for a presentation (page 127) and if you have already dealt with it in a presentation it will not be asked at the interview. There are three risks here.

> Risk 1: trying to stun the panel with the brilliance of your analysis, droning on and on for well past the three-minute limit. The impression this will give is of pomposity and vanity.

> Risk 2: you haven't done the research, so cannot answer convincingly.

> Risk 3: being sharply critical of the state of affairs you believe you would inherit in the job. This is unwise on two grounds. First you are still an outsider and your information will be partial, however well you have done your research. Then, the people doing the hiring have probably had a major hand in creating whatever the problems are. They do not therefore want to hear from you, a mere candidate and an outsider, how they have got everything wrong.

As part of my pitch to a market research company, they had asked me to critique their website. This was the topic of my presentation. I did exactly what they said and spent hours analyzing it. The site was pretty poor – several spelling or punctuation mistakes, many of the links didn't work and visually it was very dull. When they told me I hadn't got the job and I asked why, the feedback was that I had been 'rude and insensitive' in my comments. It took me a long time to accept that although they said they wanted to know what was wrong with the website, they didn't really want to hear it or at least not in the way I put it.

How to answer

Stress the tentative nature of your suggestions. Concentrate on what might be achieved in future rather than dwelling too heavily on the weaknesses of the present. Choose some kind of simple framework for the reply: for instance, two major external challenges (political change perhaps, or competitor activity), two internal ones (creating a new team, getting better relationships with a rival department). Alternatively choose short-, medium- and longer-term challenges, blending internal and external. For each of the challenges, add a few sentences setting out how you would start the process of dealing with them, making clear that you know it would look different once you were in the job.

The competency questions

With well trained interviewers, this should take up the bulk of the time. There will be no mystery about the competencies. They will have been listed in the person specification already sent to you. For almost all jobs, typical competencies will be: teamwork; customer/client focus; persuasiveness; communication (written and oral); problem solving; IT literacy. For managerial jobs you can add competencies such as: leadership; strategic thinking; managing performance, political awareness, numerical ability. A competency is the behaviour you can demonstrate reliably, time after time, underpinned by knowledge and skill (see also page 107). A competency-based interview, sometimes also described as a *behaviourally focused interview*, is an excellent way for panel and candidate to get the maximum value from the interview because it sets out to get specific evidence of real past behaviour, rather than indulging in a pointless exchange of opinions, or inviting the candidate to make unsubstantiated assertions. Asking candidates for their opinions only shows how well they can offer an opinion. Ability to engage in debating is not usually correlated with later success in the job – unless you are looking for a role as a parliamentary candidate.

Seeking evidence of past problem solving gives a firmer indication of how a candidate might behave in the future. The questioner will aim to help you by starting the question with 'Can you give us an example of a time when you had to . . . <influence a more senior colleague; make a difficult decision under extreme time pressure; challenge a team member who was under-performing>.' A competency-based interview may sometimes be carried out as part of the assessment centre, where it would not be uncommon for the interview to explore all the competencies listed and could therefore take up to 90 minutes: an exceptionally thorough process. If it is part of a panel interview, it would be normal for a selected range of competencies to be chosen; so for instance, persuasiveness and influencing skill might have been assessed earlier in the process and it would be unusual for these to be probed again at the interview.

Magic answers: the enormous importance of storytelling in dealing with these questions

The secret here is to use the surprisingly neglected principle of storytelling, and I believe that it is one of the main reasons that around 70% of my clients get the jobs they apply for. This is why it works.

The human brain is hard-wired to hear stories. Long before we could read and write as a species we must have told stories. It was the way the history of the tribe was passed through the generations, it was the way religious beliefs were affirmed, it was one of the ways children were socialized, it was the way people were entertained – and still is. We love narrative. We can't get enough of it. Think of it like this: the interview is a social event, the panel are your hosts and you are the guest. The role of a guest is to enter fully into the spirit of the event and to entertain. The panel will usually be spending a full day on the stressful and potentially boring task of interviewing. Although mostly they will be doing their best to manage it, they may be tired and crabby before it is even half way through. A candidate who keeps them awake and interested has more than just a slight advantage. Also, by being engaging, you will be answering one of the panel's unspoken but most important questions: do I like this person enough to want to work with them?

To use this approach, you first need to understand how stories are structured. All stories whether films, novels, plays or children's fairy tales have these four elements:

1. Things are going along apparently fine.
2. There is a crisis, the hero or heroine is faced with a challenge. The consequences of not dealing with it could be disastrous. Will he or she be able to overcome whatever it is, mentally or physically?
3. What the hero or heroine actually does to overcome the difficulties.
4. The happy or unhappy ending.

Authors often play with these elements – for instance, starting with the ending, or using flashbacks. Many films, plays and novels contain a rhythm of several cycles of the storytelling format, ending with one major crisis. For job interview purposes, you need to use the simple, linear format above. In effect, your answers to the competency questions are like a string of storytelling beads, threaded throughout the interview, each a precious, tightly-packed mini-story taking, remember, no longer than three minutes to tell.

Here is an example of how it could work in practice. Angela is competing for the job of PA to a Chief Executive. She already has experience as PA to a Director but the new job is in a larger organization and involves more responsibility.

Her interviewer asks: *This job needs a high level of organizing ability. Have you got that?*

Unasked question: *Are you organized enough to deal with the myriad demands that come into the Chief Executive's office? Can you take the pressure?*

Angela has already prepared thoroughly. She knows she will be asked this question because it is on the list of essential skills the successful candidate must have. This is how she replies:

	Comments
Yes I have! I pride myself on being able to organize the busiest office. So if I can give you an example . . .	*She acknowledges the interviewer's actual question and then swings straight into story mode*
Last Thursday was a very demanding day. I knew my boss had several tough meetings ahead and I'd planned to get there half an hour before him and had his files ready to take into the meetings.	*Phase 1: things going along as expected*
But then he called me from the car to say that the Chairman wanted an urgent meeting to deal with a leaked story about a safety recall on a product <she describes it> – you might have seen it in the press – and the Chairman has a reputation for being a bit of a stickler for protocol, so all my plans for the day were suddenly upended and there was the distinct possibility of confusion and anxiety everywhere.	*Phase 2: crisis; she spells out the consequences of not dealing with it.* *This takes about 30 seconds to describe*
So I had to quickly get on the phone and call all the colleagues who'd have been at the meetings and re-arrange, as otherwise there would have been chaos, and I cancelled the catering. I called my boss back to consult him about priorities for the postponed meetings. Then I set about contacting the other PAs to reinstate the most important meeting, following this up with emails. Meanwhile there were dozens of panicky phone calls from people wanting to know what was going on and wanting to talk to my boss, so I had to give them a précised version and discuss confidentiality with them too and decide who really needed to talk to him direct. The Press office were also on to me to check on his whereabouts. <She describes how she dealt with them>. I arranged a protected half hour period to call them all back <she describes more examples of staying calm and organized in this period>. I also realized that the	*Phase 3: what she did: this takes up around 1½ minutes of her answer*

179

team would be worried, so I devoted another period to calling and emailing them to say that X <boss> would be coming back in the early afternoon after the press conference and booking the room for the meeting. I was in constant touch with X via text on our BlackBerries as I was aware how stressful all of this would be for him and wanted to give him my best support.

By the end of the day I was proud of what I'd achieved: I'd got all the meetings in diaries, stayed calm and had also managed to get everything ready for Friday.

Phase 4: the happy ending

Angela has skilfully woven her own behaviour inside a dramatic story, hinting at two other characters, her boss and the Chairman, demonstrating amply that she does plan carefully and that she can stay calm and organized in difficult circumstances.

Preparation, not rehearsal

It may seem a bit of a hair-splitting point, but preparation is not the same as rehearsal. Rehearsal implies learning answers by rote: never a good idea as you will seem stiff and unnatural and could get flustered if you lose your way in your 'script'. There is no point in rehearsing answers to questions as you can never guess or control how the panel are going to phrase their questions. If you rehearse, you will answer the question you wish or think you ought to have been asked and this will mightily annoy the interviewers. Rehearsal stops you thinking on your feet and listening carefully to the question. However, there is every point in preparing. Take the competency list and write down each competency or quality on a large piece of paper. For each one, think

- What are my best examples of times when I have shown I can do this? The best example will be the one where there was most at stake.
- How can I create a story around each of them?

- How can I sketch in the characters involved?
- What real obstacles did I have to overcome? How did I overcome each one?
- What evidence can I give of the happy ending? The more tangible the proof, the better the story will be.

For each competency it will be sensible to prepare at least two stories. This enables you to stay flexible and to use any one of your bank of stories depending on how the interviewer asks the question. So for instance, Angela's anecdote about the day a product-recall wrecked her plans could just as well have been used as a good answer to a question about how she responds to stress, or to how a PA should best support a boss.

The strengths and weaknesses questions

These questions have become clichés and even the most unsophisticated employer is now unlikely to ask them straight out. Common variants are

What would your biggest fans say about you?

What would your sternest critics say?

What are you most proud of in the last year? What's the most important thing you've learnt?

What's the biggest mistake you've made in the last year?

The unasked question is this: *How self-aware are you?*

Answering the strengths question

This is not the moment for false modesty – a little boasting is invited and expected. Prepare for this question in advance by asking yourself

- What do people constantly say they admire about me?
- What am I most proud of in the last year?

181

- What have I always been able to do easily and well that other people seem to find hard?
- What skills do I know I have that this job definitely needs?

If you are asked for an example of a specific achievement, then use the competency-based, storytelling format I describe on page 178. The simplest answers are often the best, for instance to begin with, *I'm proud of the way I . . .* Another effective way to answer this question is to quote others: for instance describing what your boss has said in your last appraisal, or what colleagues spontaneously congratulate you on. Or if you have had a 360 feedback report, you will have ample evidence of what people value in you as a colleague.

> *In my recent 360 report, I was touched to see that what people like about working with me is that I'm good at coming up with innovative solutions to problems. I think it's true because I love brainstorming and working with a team. I'm at my best when all the obvious answers aren't right and there's nothing sparks me off like getting together with a group and coming up with better solutions than anyone first thought of. So an example would be the time when <then you give a story example>.*

The ideal answer will have two parts: strengths that are needed in the job and personality characteristics that are also an asset.

How to answer the weakness question

You need to avoid the mistake of appearing to think you are flawless, answering for instance as one candidate did by saying coyly, 'That's for you to find out'. No one is perfect, so the instant judgement of the interviewer will be that you are chronically lacking in self-awareness. Another self-imposed ambush is of offering something so trivial that it also conveys that you believe yourself to be faultless. If you are blazingly honest about what you believe to be a chronic weakness, you may rule yourself out if this is something that could be interpreted as damaging for those working with you. The best option is careful honesty: the potential we all have

Strength	How overdoing it becomes a weakness
Being able to see the bigger picture	Not good at detail
Perfectionism	Finding it difficult to delegate
	Driving people too hard
Strong work ethic	Getting tired and ratty

for over-using a strength so that it becomes a weakness. Some examples might be

However, the real point here is about how you manage the weakness. So if your strength is in big-picture thinking, something you already know is needed for the job, you might say

> *I think there's a flip side to my interest in seeing the big picture and this is that I know I'm not good at everyday detail. I can do it when it's really important but I know I need people alongside me to remind me, prompt me and handle the detail that I can safely ignore. So I've learnt over the years how important a good PA is to me in doing that* <you give an example, using story-telling format>.

This answer reassures the questioner: you know you can get lost in the detail but you also know how to work with others in order to balance that weakness. Note that even if the question invites you to name multiple weaknesses, one example is always enough.

The personal circumstances question

It is against the law for an interviewer to ask you questions which are discriminatory. These include questions about your marital status, sexual orientation, religious beliefs, childrearing arrangements, health or financial status, political views. Nonetheless, canny employers have ways of asking you to divulge such information and very occasionally you might meet an employer so antediluvian that they are unaware that these are questions they should not ask.

183

The asked question might be

> *This job is based in Southampton and I see from your CV that you live in Yorkshire. Does that present any difficulty for you?*
>
> *This job involves at least 80 days a year out of the UK. How does that seem?*
>
> *We sometimes need to do long days here with an 8 am start . . .*
>
> *Anyone doing this job needs to be capable of walking about five miles a day. Are you up to that?*
>
> *We're looking for someone to give us unbroken service for three years. How does that play with you?*

The unasked questions are: *do you have childcare problems? Will your partner refuse to move? Can you cope with the mental and physical stresses of this job? Are you likely to get pregnant? Are you gay?*

It never pays to bridle or take offence, even if you are actually offended. I once saw an interviewer blurt out, most unwisely, a question about the candidate's on-going divorce, something she had disclosed on her CV. She flushed angrily, gave a haughty reply saying that she didn't think he should have asked that question, and in fact refused to answer. There was an embarrassed pause while the interviewer looked helplessly around the room hoping someone would rescue him. He later acknowledged, with mortification, that he should not have asked the question, but his pride was piqued by the reproach and although she was a strong candidate she did not get the job.

The best tactic is to anticipate the question. You should expect to be asked about anything you have put on your CV or application form. If in fact there is something about the job that means that your personal circumstances would prevent you doing it on the terms described then you should not be applying. No employer is going to be pleased if, after they have offered you the job, it turns out that you can only work from 10 till 4 because you have to collect your child from school, or that you have a chronic health

184

condition which means you have frequent hospital appointments. Always explore in advance how far these constraints would be acceptable to the employer and, if the answer is that they would not be, then you should withdraw your application.

Assuming that there are no such problems, then the best way to answer is with reassurance by giving whatever brief information you feel comfortable to disclose at this point.

> *Foreign travel is fine by me. I do it in my current job and I'm single so there are no problems to sort out at home, other than arranging a cat-sitter!*
>
> *I have two young children and an excellent live-in nanny so occasional long days are not a problem for me*
>
> *My plan would be to commute weekly and to use the time to look around for a house and school rather than making the move straight away*
>
> *My partner (sex carefully unidentified) is self-employed in IT and can work from anywhere*

The personal qualities questions

These are usually listed on the person specification. Popular qualities that all employers seek include being self-motivated, resilient and self-confident. In fact these questions are variants either of the strengths and weaknesses questions or of the competency questions and can be answered in the same way. The question may be put like this:

> *What would an ideal day be for you?*
>
> *What would your day from hell be?*
>
> *What kind of person would count as your ideal boss?*
>
> *What kind of person would be your nightmare boss?*

The unasked questions are: *Are you flaky? How needy are you? Do you crumble under pressure?*

The best answer is to use a story, as described earlier, introducing it by giving a brief answer to the question and then signalling your intention to tell a story around it.

> *An ideal day for me is one where I go home at the end of it feeling that I've progressed all my main projects. So, if I can give you an example, Wednesday last week was exactly such as day when I . . .*

The 'what questions do you have for us?' question

This wraps up the interview as far as the interviewers are concerned. They are already looking at their watches and getting anxious about possibly over-running. Their attention is drifting to the next candidate. Here is what not to do:

> We were interviewing for a trainer to join our team. She'd done a pretty good interview but then, in the final question about her questions for us, she turned to me and started interrogating me. What were my own qualifications? How good a boss did I consider myself to be? What was my management style? It was so inappropriate and embarrassing. She looked all set to graunch on for another 15 minutes but fortunately my HR person intervened and said firmly, 'Thank you, X, but I'm afraid we don't have time for a long conversation now. If we offer you the job perhaps it's a theme you could take up informally.' Naturally I did not want someone so tactless on my staff.

The truth is that this question is just a ritual courtesy. You should have a few questions up your sleeve, though most probably all your questions will already have been answered earlier in the process. But choose from

Questions about priorities in the job	What is the most important target for the successful candidate to hit in their first six months?
Questions about how much autonomy you would have	How much freedom would the successful candidate have to appoint their own team? Where would the boundaries be between this role and yours?
Questions about the selection process	What's the next step in the selection process? How soon will you be letting us know about your decision? And how?

You can also use those final moments to reinforce your answer to the why you want the job question, offering the interviewers a capsule version of your skills and your strong wish to do the job.

Telephone interviews

These may be done at the initial selection stage as a cheap and swift way of screening people, or they may be done because candidates are in different countries and time zones. There is no getting around the fact that you are at a disadvantage because the interviewer is deprived of so much data about you. You need to prepare every bit as carefully as you would for a face-to-face occasion. Never conduct such a conversation in your jeans or pyjamas: dress formally because it will make a difference to how you feel. Double check the time of the call and time-zone differences. Get all the relevant papers together and spread them out on a desk in front of you. Make sure that your children and pets are well out of the way and that you have complete privacy. Don't have any water or coffee available as the noise of slurping will be clearly heard as will any random keyboard tapping in which you engage during the interview. Sit up, smile while you're talking. Give the interviewer a back-up number for you in case the planned connection fails for some reason.

If the interview is conducted via video conferencing or Skype then avoid stripes or spots which can strobe, and also dense blacks and greys as these will make you appear as a big dark blob. Highly saturated bright colours like red can also 'bleed'. Avoid stark white for the same reason. Check how you look against your background, so if your background colour is blue, avoid dressing in blue as you will disappear.

Otherwise, treat the interview in exactly the same way as outlined in this chapter.

Two final points

I not we

Modesty sometimes leads candidates to understate their own role in a story describing their achievements. They will talk about 'we'. This leaves the interviewer baffled. Who is 'we'? Always make it clear what actual role you played, acknowledging the part that others contributed. So it is fine to say

> *I decided to take that course of action <you have described it> and then made sure that the team carried it out*

> *My role was to coordinate our response working closely with my colleagues*

As I write this I have just come from a coaching session with a new client, going through a detailed feedback report on his dismally disappointing failure to win a place on an important development programme for which he is amply qualified. The report contains phrases like

> 'X failed to say how he was personally involved in the project . . .' 'X constantly used *We* not *I* and this left us unclear about his role . . .' . . . 'once again X talked about "the team" in vague terms and we did not know what unique contribution he'd made.'

For this client, learning how to claim proper credit for his achievements will be an important part of our work together.

Practising

One of the most important ways of ensuring that you perform well at the interview is to have a practice role play with a friend or family member who is wholly on your side and can be guaranteed to give you honest feedback. The feedback-giver does not need to know anything at all about the job. Just give them this book and ask them to formulate their own questions around each of the topics in this chapter – and the next. Stop after each question and ask for comment: *how does that seem to you? What came across strongly? What could I improve?* Ask for feedback on body language as well as on content. Where there are improvement areas, have another try. Just doing this makes a huge difference: you have a first attempt at framing your answers and the chance to assess how well you are striking someone who is on your side but also prepared to be ruthlessly honest. This is much better than doing it for the first time at the actual interview.

Hold in mind the work/life balance

Or in any contradiction of the panel members

Stay alert to the underlying unasked questions

And at no time answer with an untruth

Indulge in no criticism of my present boss

According to the Geneva Convention I need only supply my name, rank and number

12 ANSWERING TRICKY QUESTIONS

> **Myth**: Interviewers are impulsive or volatile and might throw you an unanswerable question just to catch you out
>
> **Reality**: you can usually prepare for the seemingly 'tricky' questions

Tricky questions are mostly totally predictable. Interviewers will always spot obvious problems from your CV, for instance gaps in employment, and will ask you about them. You can therefore prepare your answers confidently.

The unasked question is always: *is there some problem about this person that we should know about?*

In general, the principles are

- Never lie: it is increasingly common for organizations to check up on qualifications with awarding bodies. All employers will also be likely to ask a previous employer to confirm your job title, salary and dates of employment.
- Where this is something that could be a disadvantage to your bid for the job, give the version of the truth which is least damaging to you.
- Don't apologize unnecessarily: redundancy, unfortunately, is a frequent interruption to careers and most people now understand that it is the job that is terminated not the person.
- Never criticize your current or last job, boss and organization even if you parted on difficult terms. Always stress what you enjoyed about your previous work.
- Never argue with a panel member about whether or not some aspect of your career is a disadvantage – e.g. whether if you have an arts degree you would be able to deal with scientists.

Here are some of the most common challenging questions with suggestions about how to reply:

Question	Suggested approach to replying
You lack some qualification that people in this job usually have – e.g. did not go to university	Explain straightforwardly why this happened – e.g. family circumstances and that your record proves you can handle the work as ably as anyone with the qualification
You have had a long career break while you reared your children	Emphasize what you have learnt from this and the organizational skills you have acquired; describe how you have kept up your professional interests
You have had serious health problems	Describe how you have recovered and are now fully fit
There is a criminal conviction in your past	It is a spent conviction, you have paid your debt and have been a model citizen for x years; it was a youthful mistake that you regret
You have moved around a lot – often a problem with young graduates	You have deliberately given yourself a period of temp jobs, travelling and studying to broaden your outlook and are now fully ready to settle down
You have been in the same organization for a long time	Acknowledge that this might be seem to be a problem but stress the interest your jobs held for you, the different roles you have had in that time, that you have kept your skills fresh by taking advantage of any training and development on offer and how easy it will be for you to adapt

You are openly invited to criticize your current or immediately past employer.

The question might be put as *'What's the worst thing about your present job and organization?'*

Sometimes intended as a deliberate trap to test your discretion and loyalty, this question is most often asked, in my experience, when two organizations are competitors. Jealousy or an impulsive wish to conduct a little light espionage then overwhelms the interviewer. Keep your answer brief and courteous, putting the spotlight on you rather than on the organization. This candidate was looking for a job at a rival company in the hospitality sector. Note how carefully and tactfully she steered her way around the invitation to be critical of her current organization, without putting the interviewer down for asking such a dubious question.

> That's quite difficult to answer because there's nothing truly bad about either my job or the organization. I have really loved my job, it's given me all kinds of opportunities and the organization is great – it took me in as a raw beginner and has invested a lot in my development. But as you know it's relatively small and we've got a very flat organization structure. When I came into the job the directors were very clear that the most they really expected people to stay was four years because there's no natural way of getting promotion. I've now done three of those four years and it does feel like it's time to move on – some of the challenge has gone out of the work for me because it's become routine and I want more responsibility on a wider range of projects than we typically have. And in fact they are supporting me wonderfully in my job search even though I know they'd really like me to stay.

When you have left under difficult circumstances

If you are unemployed, the trickiest question of all is to be asked why you left your last job. The general principles here are

● To keep your answer short and straightforward.
● To stay calm and pleasant: never betray any anger.
● To tell a version of the truth which is most favourable to you and to avoid lying. When a potential future employer scents a problem, the first thing he or she will do is to call your previous boss. This call will probably include the question, 'Would you employ him/her again?' So if you bend the truth, the chances of discovery are high.

● Be discreet about the former employer: the correct attitude is that you wish them well. Keep any sense of blame out of your answers.

If the loss of your job was straightforwardly because the company was shedding jobs as a response to economic difficulties then the answer is easy. You keep it crisp, short and simple.

> My company was supplying local authorities with <you describe it>. Our clients had huge cuts of 30% in their budgets and our business fell away dramatically. We had no option but to cut our staff as well and unfortunately my job was one of the ones the axe fell on, along with 25 others.

This makes it clear that there was nothing personal in the loss of your job. Avoid sounding bitter or resentful as you describe what happened. The best attitude to convey is a calm, mature, 'these things happen'.

If you took voluntary redundancy because you had become a bit stale in the job, then there is a reliable variant:

> My company was supplying local authorities with <you describe it>. Our clients had huge cuts of 30% in their budgets and our business fell away dramatically. The executive team offered staff the chance to bid for voluntary redundancy and I jumped at it. I'd been there for eight years and felt it was time to move on and was lucky enough to have my bid accepted.

This version stresses that it was entirely your choice to make the move, but you describe it enthusiastically in a way that does so without blaming the employer for creating a 'boring' or 'unchallenging' environment – in other words you take responsibility for yourself, something every employer admires and wants.

Let's suppose that there is a not so happy story behind leaving your job. The real reason you left was that you were sacked for poor performance after a drawn-out disciplinary process or after a series of disputes with your boss. How you answer this question will depend on what you and your former employer have agreed about the official reasons for your departure, and whether or not they have agreed to supply a reference.

These are examples of how some people have successfully answered this question:

Matthew was forced out of his job after a new Chief Executive took over the small independent TV company where he worked. A bid for a large piece of work with a major broadcaster failed and the CEO blamed Matthew. This was the trigger for a conversation which led to his leaving.

> I left the firm because when X <new CEO> took over we had very different views about the strategy. He also wanted to assume responsibility for parts of my role and these unfortunately were the ones that I most enjoyed doing <he briefly describes them>. So it was clear there wasn't room for both of us and we agreed that I would leave.

Comment: everything in the above was true and faithfully mirrored the official story about Matthew's departure. It omits any reference to the failed piece of work, and implies that it was a mutual decision, whereas the truth was that it was not. It also rings true because all recruiters know that the arrival of a new boss is frequently followed by the departure of senior members of the inherited team and does not necessarily reflect badly on the person who is leaving.

197

There were changes in the way we had to respond to legislation <candidate describes them briefly> and that meant we were restructured. My skills lie in <she describes them> and the new structure meant that the department needed people who could <she describes the new skills the department needed> and this was not me. So I came to an agreement with my boss that I would leave.

Alternatives

I completed my Occupational Psychology MA two years ago and that was a turning point for me. It gave me a lot of confidence in my own abilities and also developed my interest in organizational change. There are really no opportunities in my present job to work on this except in a very junior role and I felt I had to make some kind of total break with the past – I think when you've been in a humble role in a company it's inevitable that they see you like that – it's hard for everyone to appreciate that you've grown. But in any case there was a real mismatch between the skills I now want to use and the chances to use them, and that's why I left.

Comment: these accounts could conceal a painful and drawn-out process where the person concerned has been the subject of a *capability review* or a disciplinary process of some kind and found wanting. However, presenting it calmly and confidently minimizes the chances of the new employer probing too much. Also what is on your side here is that when a potential employer really likes what they see in you, they are often inclined to conclude that your previous employer was 'dim' or 'stupid' and that their own judgement is superior.

198

When you've been unemployed for a long time

The suspicion in the interviewer's mind is that there is some problem about you and that possibly you are unemployable. The employer may also believe, with some justification, that people who have been unemployed for a long time get used to dossing about and may find it hard to settle back into the routines of work. At times of high unemployment, this matters less because it is more common for many people to be out of work for longish periods of time.

How to answer:

- You say that you have taken advantage of the loss of your job to re-think your career and that you have been in no rush to leap into a new job for the sake of it
- You describe the many fulfilling activities in which you have taken part, stressing achievements, especially any that involve leading and organizing
- You emphasize the care you have taken to focus on getting the kind of job that will fit with your life as it is now
- You describe any training you have done while out of work
- You stress your commitment to hard work and discipline

It was a shock to lose my job and I spent about three weeks feeling numb, but that soon passed and I came to see it as a good chance to think hard about what I wanted to do next. I've always been interested in teaching as a career and I've spent the last year starting and running an informal mentoring scheme for young people on my estate and also a community campaign to get our community centre open again – this has been really successful and I heard yesterday that the Council has agreed to do it. Now I'm totally clear that I want to retrain as a teacher so I'm looking for this job as a classroom assistant as a way of getting myself ready for a formal application to the university next September through proper experience in a school like yours which specializes in the arts, as that's my own specialist area. I'm really wanting to buckle down and get going and I love the idea of working in a disciplined way in a tightly managed school like this one.

Questions about salary and benefits

It is only the most clumsy interviewer who asks these questions during the interview because the interview is neither the place nor the time to have the discussion. The excitement and stress of the interview makes it difficult to give a thought-through answer and the actual negotiation will depend on benefits other than salary (see page 215). If you are asked a question such as 'What salary do you expect?' use replies like this:

> *I'd much rather save the answer until both you and I are clear that I'm the right person for the job*

Or

> *I'm sure you pay a fair rate for the job depending on people's experience and skill*

Stress that the fit of the job is the most important criterion for you at this stage. If you are asked about your current salary, reply straightforwardly but remember to include and explain the value of the total benefits package.

When you are applying for a job at a much lower salary than you previously earned

In times of economic hardship and retraction, many job-seekers are forced to consider jobs at lower salaries and with far less responsibility. The question in the employer's mind is whether you are serious, whether perhaps you are over-qualified and therefore whether you will move on too soon, or behave in a self-important way that will alienate colleagues. One of my former clients faced this possible doubt in an interviewer's mind when his organization was merged and his job disappeared. In his sessions with me it became clear that he no longer wanted a senior role. He did want a local job with more limited responsibility and did not need the large salary he had been earning before, as his material wants were few. He was applying for a job at less than half his previous salary and in the same sector. This is how he prepared the answer to the question he was indeed asked: *Why would you take this when it's so much more junior and less well paid than your previous role?*

> I was 50 two months ago and that birthday has caused me to rethink what I want out of life. I did love my last job but I've absolutely no wish to find another one like it. I realize you might be wondering why, but it's all about finding a balance between work and family. I typically work very hard and would in this job, but I no longer want the travel, the weekends taken up entirely by work, and I never needed the big salary. This job attracts me because it's in the same field, and would allow me to offer you my skills. I want to go back to hands-on operational work because that's what I think I'm good at. I would bring you my knowledge and experience, I could walk to work and still have time to see my wife!

This statement must have been convincing as he was offered the job and is still doing it happily.

Emergency rescue

You need to observe the panel's attentiveness throughout. If they are losing interest in you this will show in their body language: crossed arms, twirled hair, yawns, slumped posture, gazing down at their notes, fiddling with papers, waggling feet. Usually it is too late by the time you have noticed these signs. But it is worth trying for a last minute rescue:

- Up your own energy dramatically: raise your voice, smile.
- Consider whether it is possible that some specific recent answer has switched them off. If so, it's worth asking: 'I'm wondering if there was something in my answer to that question that has struck the wrong note?'
- If challenged on an opinion you have given, don't suddenly panic and offer a blander version as this will look craven and will undermine your credibility.
- High risk option: consider saying as your closing statement, *I'm aware I seem to have lost your interest and I'm wondering what I can do to reassure you that I'm still very interested in this job and convinced that I can do it.*

Problem interviewers

If only life was perfect and every interviewer was trained, competent and charming. But sadly it is not. Some interviewers are untrained, incompetent and rude. What do you do if you encounter one?

Interviewer asks hypothetical questions or invites you to give an opinion

The untrained and incompetent interviewer adores hypothetical questions. 'What would you do if some unbelievably awful event happened?' (which they describe). Such questions are virtually always about a crisis. The hidden question is about what you would do in an emergency.

The reasons these are terrible questions are that the crisis would never happen exactly like this in real life and the sensible solution will depend on what was happening at the time. The answer may also depend on knowledge of emergency procedures which, as a candidate, you are unlikely to have, and the answer only tests how a candidate would answer a hypothetical question – which may be totally different from what they would do in real life.

I coached a very young friend applying for a vacation job in a care home and showed her how to answer such a question. When it was asked it was, 'What would you do if a resident locked himself into his room and threatened to set fire to it?' Emma described how she had previously dealt capably with a similar though not identical emergency. She got the job but was later teased by the boss who had asked this absurd question, and whose comment was, 'Of course we always have duplicate keys, so you could just open the door'. There was no way Emma could have known this without being on the staff.

The way to answer is

● Acknowledge the question briefly: talk about how you would stay calm and ascertain the facts before rushing to action; mention that you would already make sure you were familiar with emergency procedures; say that you would do everything feasible to prevent such an occurrence happening.
● Swing into story-mode, giving an example of a time when you handled something as near as possible like the crisis your interviewer describes.

Other scenarios involving incompetent interviewers

Mostly these people have no idea of their incompetence. This does not mean that they are poor managers or bad people, only that they most probably have never been trained. At its extreme they may be like the client of a colleague who had hired her to help select a new team and alleged that he had second sight where people were concerned; he could tell instantly whether they were '30 watt people or 200 watt people'. The only problem was that this amazing gift did not seem to correlate with his success at keeping them in his department because no sooner had the 200 watt people been appointed than many of them upped and went elsewhere, which did not say much for his superpowers at selecting them or possibly for his skills as a manager.

An incompetent interviewer may do any of the following: just seems to want a chat; launches into a long account of the history of the company and their starring role in it; asks rude and provocative questions such as 'Why on earth should I appoint someone like you? Or 'Your psychometrics show someone who's totally bananas'; seems sleepy and disengaged; allows the interview to be constantly interrupted by flunkeys who rush in with 'important' messages.

An interviewer who asks rude questions is sometimes deluded into thinking that when subjected to 'stress', people will reveal their 'true' selves or how they respond to criticism. You may want to think twice or three times about whether you want to work with someone who behaves like this. Assuming that you do, the best tactics are to

- Stay calm, smile, avoid getting defensive.
- Ask for more clarification about the question: *When you say my psychometrics may show someone totally bananas, which aspects were you thinking of?*
- Keep your replies brief.

With all the other scenarios you will have to take control of the interview and ask the interviewer what they are looking for and what skills the appointed person will need. You then make statements and tell the stories that answer the questions you *should* have been asked. One of my clients, faced with a flustered interviewer who was continually interrupted by phone calls, said sympathetically and politely, 'It seems this may not be an ideal time for us to talk, should we fix another time?' only to have the interviewer jerk to attention as if coming out of a dream, and say, 'No, no, I really want to talk to you', rush out and instruct his PA to guarantee silence from the phones and have the conversation that he should have organized in the first place.

Finally

You are still on show while you are in the building, so leave any 'phew, glad that's over' calls to your family and friends, or gasps at cigarettes, until the whole event is over and you are well outside and unobserved.

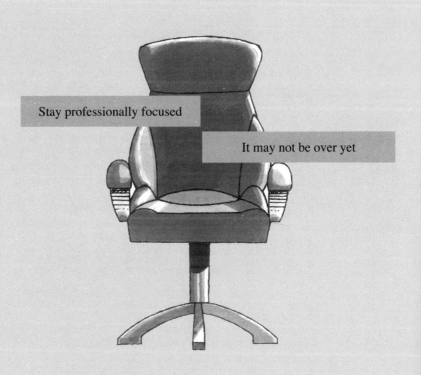

13 AFTER THE INTERVIEW

> **"** **Myth**: after the interview it's all in the employer's hands
>
> **Reality**: there's a lot that any candidate can do to further their own cause **"**

Immediate follow-up

Regardless of how well or badly you think it has gone, you must write a letter of thanks immediately. By a letter, I mean a snail-mail letter, not an email. Real letters written on paper and posted in a handwritten envelope now have extraordinary power because they are so rare. Write to the person on the panel who will be making the decision – this is normally the person who would be your line manager if you got the job. The reasons for doing this are that few people do, so it gives you an edge and it also allows you to restate your interest in the job. If there was some important piece of data that you forgot in all the stress of the interview, then you can add it, very briefly.

How to write it

Choose the paper carefully. It should be A4 100 gsm 'laid' paper, in white or very pale cream with a matching envelope.

- Head the letter with the name of the job.
- Address them as Dear Ms or Mr unless you are certain you have permission to use a first name.
- Double check the spelling of the person's name and also check whether they have titles, honours or degrees that they attach to their name. If they do, this will normally be on the paperwork you have been sent by the company.
- First paragraph: thanks them for seeing you and says that you enjoyed the process.
- Second paragraph: confirms your interest in the job, says that the selection process has deepened your understanding of what it would involve and then gives a summary in no more than thirty words of why you feel you would be a good choice.
- Final paragraph: says that you will call them in three days to find out how things stand.

209

- Get a pedantic friend to read the whole thing before you send it: a misplaced apostrophe or clumsy misspelling could undermine the impression you want to give.
- End it with *Yours sincerely*. Write the salutation and the sign-off by hand, but print everything else in a 12 point standard typeface, non-italic version, such as Times New Roman or Arial. Address the envelope by hand, labelling it *Personal and Confidential* – this will ensure that it reaches the addressee.

The longer the time interval between the interview and no news, the less likely it is that you are the chosen candidate, unless you know that the interview process is being spread over a period of time. Panels usually make up their minds on the day and immediately phone the successful candidate for a verbal agreement, subject to satisfactory references and sometimes to medical checks. The unsuccessful candidates are contacted after that. When you don't hear anything and there is a mysterious silence, the usual reason is that the favourite candidate is haggling over money or about release from their current job and the panel is hedging its bets, especially if you are the runner-up. The other possible scenario is that the panel cannot agree – it is a 'hung panel' and a bit like a hung parliament this is an uncomfortable and unsatisfactory state, making decisive choice difficult. It can also happen that the panel does not rate any of the people it saw and is going to return to the long list to see whether it might have missed a strong candidate. Sometimes the panel decides on its favourite but has to refer the decision to a more senior person. Occasionally this senior person will veto the choice and this throws the whole process into chaos, which may take days if not weeks to resolve. Sometimes the organization is careless and inefficient or can't be bothered to let the unsuccessful candidates know their fate, in which case you are well shot of them.

If three days have passed and you have heard nothing, call the HR person who will most probably have chaired the panel. Your dialogue goes like this:

Introduce yourself, name the job and remind him or her that you were a candidate for it.

Ask politely if a decision has been made. If it's a 'no' for you, you will be told at this point. If there is still some uncertainty, the HR person may hint at what this is. Don't press for clarity on the reasons but do ask when the uncertainty is likely to be resolved. If you have another interview or even better, an actual job offer from another employer, then now is the time to say so, explaining that it would be helpful to know where you stand. Ask if you may call again.

If it's a turndown

It is not a tragedy if you fail to get the job, even though it can often seem as if it is. Typically we feel any mixture of bruised, angry, humiliated, disappointed and tearful. These are symptoms of rejection and there is no getting away from it, rejection has happened. Allow yourself to feel the hurt for a few hours and confide in your stoutest supporter. Let this person comfort you with soothing balm about how it's the employer's loss, they are stupid not to have seen your quality – and so on.

Beware of believing that the interview was a set-up. This can be a temptation when you learn that the successful candidate was the in-house darling and you were a mere external competitor. A strong internal candidate is always the best bet for an employer: they are a known quantity with proven track record so it would be amazing and also unfair if they did not start as the benchmark. But remember that the in-house candidate is also likely to have obvious flaws which may be getting in the way of a promotion and many such candidates have told me that they feel they are being interviewed for purely cynical reasons, which they sometimes are. Nonetheless, I have often seen the assumed person in pole position unseated by an external candidate who did a brilliant interview or vice versa where the assumed in-house lame duck has demonstrated how exceptional they would be if offered the job. This can happen even where, secretly, the appointing line manager has already apparently decided whom he or she will appoint.

It keeps up your spirits and your reputation if you handle yourself with dignity in public after such a disappointment. Moaning, whining and criticizing the panel damages one person: you. In any case, there is only a certain amount of self-pity that is useful because sooner or later you have work to do. The most immediate task is to get yourself some feedback about the interview. This has become harder as employers have grown more nervous about being sued for wrongful decisions made on the basis of prejudice. Employers have no interest in you once they have rejected you and human distaste for giving bad news also means that the task of offering people feedback falls to the bottom of the to-do list. It is easier if you are applying for an internal promotion because managers and HR professionals recognize their duty after an interview, but even when they acknowledge it, somehow, my experience is that they wriggle out of it if they can by giving feedback that is bland and meaningless.

This should not stop you trying to collect focused feedback. If you know anyone on the panel, then target them. The more views you have the better. Otherwise go for the panel chair. The chances are that you will be brushed off with platitudes such as 'If we'd had two jobs we would have given one to you' or 'You were above the line but unfortunately we had one candidate who was a little better qualified'.

Email first to ask for a scheduled telephone conversation, promising that you will take no more than ten minutes of their time.

In the conversation, put a clock where you can see it clearly because it is important to stick to your suggested time limit. Have a piece of paper and pen ready to write down everything that is said, and ask

What were your overall impressions of me in the interview?

What specifically did the successful candidate have that I lacked?

Which parts of my interview were the best from your point of view?

Which parts could I improve on?

What, specifically, would your advice be on how to do better next time?

212

Notice that these sentences press for examples and detailed information. If you are not offered this, say 'Can you give me an example?'

Never, ever, try to justify a poor performance as this will be seen as making excuses ('I'd only had two hours sleep') and especially avoid any which seem to blame them ('I had no real time to prepare for the interview because I didn't get your letter till one day before'). Never argue or fight back – your role is just to listen and clarify. Just doing this creates a powerful impression: that you are a mature, sensible person prepared to hear something uncomfortable. Most employers will be impressed and will remember you.

Thank the feedback-giver warmly because truly what they are offering you is a priceless gift.

> When I rang for feedback, I had to bite my lip several times because what I heard was so difficult to take in – for instance that my voice was too quiet for some of them to hear, and that I 'lacked interview presence' and had not answered their questions directly. But I'm so glad I did it because I then had a specific list of things to work on for the next one. It was specially hard to hear that I'd come nowhere near the top of their list and that I needed to strengthen my experience to compete more strongly another time but that gave me just the steer I needed.

Now you must write another brief letter. This time it expresses dignified disappointment, wishes them well, and also asks them to keep you in mind if other vacancies occur. When I was an employer myself, on three separate occasions, strong but unsuccessful candidates did just this and both they and I benefitted from it. One became a valued freelancer in the department I was then running, another was shortlisted again for a different job for which she was successful and the third was offered the job when the chosen candidate dropped out.

213

The feedback may reveal a number of other things. One possibility is that this was not your job and never could be, even though you were shortlisted. Perhaps the gap between the experience asked for and the experience you have or are willing to acquire is just too wide. Or it may show how near you came to getting it. The experience may have strengthened your desire for a similar job, or destroyed your motivation for good. All of this is ultimately positive. If it really was not your job then the panel were wise to reject you. If it could be your job in the future then you will have a clear map of how to improve your chances another time. It is more important to carry on than to drown in self-pity. You have been turned down for a job, that's all: it does not define your value as a human being. As a lover of dance, I am always impressed by the way professional dancers can recover quickly from an obvious and potentially catastrophic mistake such as a tumble. They leap up so very quickly that you catch your breath: *did I really see that?* Their smiles return, their performance is flawlessly resumed, the audience forgets. That's it: get yourself up, paste back the smile, move on.

You get the offer

Mostly this is a wonderful moment. You feel affirmed. Your hard work has paid off and someone wants you. But oddly enough, this is often a moment of deflation too. You may have been playing with the idea of making a move but now playtime is over and you have to decide. A job move is an upheaval and our response to major change is ambivalent – we want it but we don't. Faced with the prospect of what we will give up – and there's always something that we value that will have to go, however much we have sought and wanted the move – there is a feeling of mournfulness for the loss. When you have thoroughly explored your reasons for wanting the job in the first place (chapter 1), this phase is mercifully short.

The offer is usually made in the first instance by phone. NEVER just accept. If you do you will instantly lose all your negotiating power. Assuming that your instinct is to say yes, the correct behaviour at this stage is to say

214

I'm very interested, but I'd like to know more about what you are offering.

The employer's attitude, and indeed your own will be governed by these factors:

How much they want you

Whether there is another candidate who might just as easily be appointed if you prove too hard to please

How much you want the job

How much flexibility there really is on the employer side.

Room for manoeuvre will depend on sector and organization. As a general rule there is usually more than most employers are willing to admit at this stage. Their interest is in keeping their wage bill down. So, for instance, if there is a fixed salary and grade scale, as there often is in public sector organizations, it is usually possible to negotiate entering such a scale at its upper limits. If you have been working with a head-hunter then let them do the negotiating for you. If you are your own negotiator then ask the employer to set out their offer in writing. Remember that there is more to the benefits of a job than the salary, though many of these benefits are taxable. I have known clients so transfixed by meeting or exceeding their current salary that they have been blind to the monetary or lifestyle value of other benefits on offer.

Any written offer should make reference to all of these

Start date	Job title
Salary	Bonus scheme if any
Manager's name	Location of job
Notice period	Performance management including length of probationary period
Holiday entitlement	Hours of work
Job description	What you will be accountable for

In addition there may be a variety of other benefits on offer. These could include

Medical insurance for you	Medical insurance for your dependants	Car
Phone bills paid	Flexitime	Possibility of working from home for part of the week
Expense account	Pension	Special leave entitlements – e.g. bereavement, maternity, paternity
Training entitlements	Employee assistance programmes	Stock options
Help with re-locating	Concierge services	Subsidized restaurant
Season ticket loan	Nursery	Sabbaticals

If you are being offered an extremely senior job then you might also want to negotiate on how much freedom you will have to move people around in your new team. For instance, there may be an unsuccessful competitor lurking and likely to sulk in the team you are taking over and you may want to get agreement to moving them on. It is common for senior managers to bring their existing PAs with them to a new job. I have seen in recent years that such senior people may also make their executive coaches part of their total package and I have been flattered and amused to have been an item in these negotiations a few times.

Employers expect to negotiate, and unless you have a head-hunter acting for you, you will be your own best advocate. Never accept an offer without at least some discussion. Plan to have three items on which you will negotiate and think carefully in advance about which are absolutes for you and which could bend. It is always easier to negotiate down than up so you should have a reasonably high figure in mind as your starting point while remembering to be sensible about whatever the norm is for people at your level, age and experience.

Some useful tactics

- Never give your current salary on your CV if you can avoid it, as this may encourage the employer to offer a rate well below what they would actually be prepared to pay. Also remember that the employer will always be more interested in the value of your existing total benefits package than just the salary.
- It is better to negotiate in person than on the phone.
- Be realistic about your worth – not too cocky and not too modest. Feeling embarrassed about discussing money is fatal and will prevent you getting the package you deserve. Remember that they like you enough to be making the offer. Going back to their short list will cost effort and possibly money, so they will not want to do it.
- Be as enthusiastic and committed as you were at the interview. Imply that with goodwill on both sides you will arrive at a fair conclusion. Emphasize the common ground – you want to work for them and they want you to work for them. The discussion is about finding a solution that is right and fair for both sides.
- Stay calm and reasonable. When made an offer which you feel is a lot too low, leave a pause and say something like, 'I have to say that sounds disappointing. I really do want to say yes, but that's a lot lower than I was expecting'. After the employer responds, you might say, 'How much room is there for manoeuvre on this?'
- Never bring your personal circumstances into the discussion. If you have recently increased your mortgage or had another child, well, tough. That's your responsibility. 'Needing' to earn more is not how salaries are awarded.
- Ask the employer to name a figure first. If you are asked straight out 'What salary are you looking for?' reply by saying, 'I'd be interested in hearing from you what sort of figure you have in mind'. Remember that the first offer is normally the lowest one the employer thinks they can get away with. Alternatively say something like, 'Perhaps you'd like to name a few figures and also tell me a bit about the overall benefits package.'

- Salary negotiations are rarely successful above 5–10% of the rate that has been advertised, even when the employer has specifically said, 'More may be available for an exceptional candidate'. You will be in a stronger position to claim your unique worth if you have already been earning at or above the advertised rate and also have obvious scarcity value.

- Do your research: find out what others are paid for doing the same job, either in the company or elsewhere.

- Listen carefully to the employer's objections: explore them and show you understand them. It's not a football match where only one side can win.

- Don't get fixed on some notional round figure. After tax, a salary of £30,000 will be more or less identical to a salary of £29,000. The only difference is in your pride. Equally important: don't get too fixed on actual job titles. Is it really worth sacrificing a well paid and interesting job for the sake of having 'Senior', 'Leader', 'Chief', 'Director', 'Executive' or Head' in your title? Such titles rarely have meaning outside the organization so the impact on your personal PR and future CV is likely to be minimal.

- Be prepared to bargain for a salary review six months into the job. In effect for your first six months you are most probably formally on probation anyway. Assuming you 'pass' that successfully, you can ask for a salary review to be formally written into your initial contract.

- Consider what the lifestyle advantages are of the less tangible benefits. For instance, being able to work from home for one day a week may release you from an unpleasant commute and allow you to see your children. This may be worth considerably more to you than a small increase in salary.

- Employers are often more willing to be flexible around other benefits than around salary. This is because such benefits are easier to accommodate and hide. So for instance, it may cost a trivial amount of money to the employer to add you to their list of employees receiving health benefits, whereas there may be much stricter scrutiny about salary.

- Ask for time to consider the offer. Requesting the offer in writing is often a useful way of gaining some thinking time, but be alert to the danger of prolonging this phase. Most employers will want the deal settled within a week at the outside of making the offer. Letting it drift on may mean that the employer loses patience and withdraws the offer.

- If there is something that strikes you as dodgy in the written offer, then you should get swift legal advice from an employment specialist and, judiciously, let the employer know that you are doing this.

- Write a snail-mail and email letter confirming or rejecting the job offer.

When you reject an offer

The most likely reason for an outright rejection is that the offered salary is at the lowest level of the scale quoted, the additional benefits are unattractive and the employer has given you convincing reasons about why this cannot be improved on. Perhaps this is bureaucratic nonsense, but if it really is the case that they are unwilling to better it, then you may feel you have no option but to say no because it falls severely below the bottom line criteria you have given yourself and you have confidence that you could do better elsewhere – or do just as well by staying put. When you also have some well justified doubts about the job itself as a result of what you have found out during the selection process, then the decision may be easy. In this case, say politely but firmly that with very great regret you are saying no, but you wish them good luck in finding the right candidate.

Take off from the old job with your good reputation intact

Arrive in your new job, looking and learning

No 'talking up' the old job

Establish fast what your new boss really expects of you

14 STARTING THE NEW JOB

> **Myth**: You just get on with it
>
> **Reality**: It pays to exit the old job gracefully and to prepare carefully for the new one

Exiting with aplomb

If you can negotiate a swift exit from your old job, do so. There is often little point in working out a notice period unless you are doing the kind of work where your absence could only be covered with great difficulty. If your new organization is keen for you to start speedily then it is worth seeing if you can reduce a lengthy notice period. If you are in any kind of managerial work, people soon stop bringing their problems because they know you will not be there to see decisions through and clued-up bosses realize that it is usually better for people to leave quickly once their departure has been announced.

> I began to feel like a bit of a non-person. From more or less the day I said I was going, people stopped inviting me to meetings, my team no longer interrupted me fifteen times a day, the phone stopped ringing and the email stopped pinging. I found myself drifting around with little to do. Fortunately I had some leave to take and that brought all the drifty stuff to a welcome end.

There are bound to be regrets about leaving. There will be people you like and it can feel sad to know that it will never be quite as easy to join in banter and gossip with them again. Suddenly these people can seem like valued friends, even if reason tells you that the friendship is and always was superficial. There is comfort in the familiar, even when the familiarity is exactly what is driving you to leave. Mostly, human beings put more energy into avoiding discomfort than into moving towards the pleasure of the new, so last-minute doubts about whether you have made the right decision are common at this stage.

The point is that the formal ending – for instance, the date you will leave – and the psychological ending are two different processes. The formal ending is abrupt, an actual date, an external event. The

223

psychological ending is fuzzy because it is an internal event: it happens slowly, tailing off gradually, and it may take weeks or even months for the ending to feel accomplished.

Some sort of leaving do is one of the best ways to manage wobbles about leaving, even if the organization is too mean to pay for a proper party. The purpose of this is to mark the formal conclusion of your time in the old job. It doesn't much matter whether it is a polite little tea party or a large-scale evening event. Presenting you with a gift, a card signed by all your colleagues with touching messages about how they will miss you, nice speeches . . . it all helps you and them to understand that, yes, you really are moving on.

At the party

Never open the present immediately. If it is wrapped in multiple layers of ribbon, string, tags, bows, paper and bubble wrap it will take an age and nervousness could make you clumsy. Have a helper-figure at your side primed to receive and hold the still-wrapped present for you. This also enables you to disguise any possible disappointment or horror at the nature of the gift. You can thank people individually later, especially the person who actually did the shopping. Instead, get on with a short, prepared speech: certainly no more than five minutes as, however popular you are, no one wants to hear people droning on at a party.

> You thank them for coming
>
> Tell two funny anecdotes from your time together
>
> Say what you will specially miss about the people and the organization
>
> Say no more than two sentences about your new job – this is because there is always a little jealousy and upset about people who leave – perhaps your good fortune is a sign that the listeners, too, should be moving?
>
> Wish them well, say how much you know they will be successful in the future and promise to keep in touch

After the stressful public part of the event is over, there may be a strong temptation to get very drunk, something which it is impossible to combine with a dignified exit so is better avoided.

Leaving after redundancy or sacking

If your exit has been managed on unpleasant terms, for instance you have been made redundant or fired, then your priority is safeguarding your reputation. Remember you are moving on and you have found another job. At the point of leaving, negative feelings may still linger. You may still feel the shock and anger associated with losing your job and want to spread damaging stories about 'what really happened'. You may feel betrayed because the organization has been like a family to you and you seek support, possibly doing a little sobbing, from subordinates or other colleagues. Or you may feel that you want to avoid all of it. You don't want to cause trouble, you just want to run away and hide. None of these behaviours is good for you and all are damaging because they look unprofessional.

Instead of any of the above, it is much better to keep your true feelings to yourself and your trusted closest friends. Concoct yourself a brief script which has three parts, delivered with a smile to anyone who asks:

> Yes, you are leaving.
>
> Imply or say that you have chosen to move on, giving a vaguely plausible reason for doing so.
>
> You are looking forward to the future and to your new job which you name without giving any real details, or say you are using the time as a welcome chance to slow down for a little while and rethink your life.

You stick to this script whatever sly digs and nosy attempts at investigation those apparently sympathetic people make.

Never just slink off: this will lengthen the adjustment time. Organize yourself a party and proceed as above.

225

The in-between period

It is important to have a gap, even if only of a few days, between leaving the old job and starting the new one. This gives you time to draw breath both metaphorically and physically, to calm down, to hang loose for a little while and refresh your energy with some enjoyable and low-stress leisure activities combined with a holiday, even if this is just a long weekend. Often the actual in-between period can be several weeks or even months, including the time when you are working out your notice and have little to do. You can use some of this time fruitfully to get ready for the new role. This could include

- Visiting the office or site of the new organization and meeting future colleagues informally
- Undertaking some training relevant to the job
- Reading any documents that your new boss feels might be important as briefing
- Having an informal meeting with your predecessor in the job, if there was one and this person is willing to meet you, though they may not agree to seeing you, especially if they have left on uncomfortable terms
- Having an informal meeting, maybe over a drink or a meal, with your future boss to discuss your first few months in the job
- Continuing the research that you started as part of your preparation for the selection process.

Resist any temptation to start doing the job in any formal sense before your actual start date. You cannot make decisions, give indications of what your first steps will be – or anything else until you are actually there.

Joining

Make sure you know when and where you are expected to report for your first day. If the route is unfamiliar to you, make a practice run first: the normal first activity in a new job is a meeting with your boss and it would be embarrassing to be late. Dress formally until you get to grips with the subtleties of the dress code. You should expect to have an induction programme planned for you; a security pass; visits to whatever parts of the organization you need to understand to do your job properly and one-to-one or small group meetings with anyone who could affect your success in the role; a buddy to show you where everything is and tell you all the real rules of the culture – the ones that are never written down but which everyone knows.

It has sometimes been alleged that a high percentage of new hires fail. I have seen figures as high as 50% quoted – that is people who leave within a year of being appointed. Ruling out for the moment that mutual mistakes were made at selection, these are the common issues, with suggestions about how to avoid the difficulties – or get around them.

Feeling unconfident

Although you have the endorsement of having been chosen, it can be a shock to enter a new job in a new organization. Even if you are in a new job in the same organization, it can feel odd: people start treating you differently. Perhaps the people who were your friends and colleagues now report to you and are more wary of you. Maybe you have an unsuccessful candidate for the job who is still in the team. Rather than skirting around such issues, it is better to confront them. If you inherit a bitter and still angry competitor, then ask to meet them and discuss candidly how the two of you are going to manage the situation. Ask how they feel about reporting to you. If the other person cannot adjust then it is probably best for them to leave or to move to another department. Where this is the case, put it on the list of topics to discuss with your boss.

When you are a newcomer to the organization, feeling uncertain and perhaps a little ungrounded, there can be a strong temptation to talk about your old job and organization as a way of reminding yourself and telling others that you do know what you are doing because you did it in your previous role. Unfortunately this will look like bragging and will also imply that you think your old place was better. It has infinite power to annoy, so don't do it.

Seeing the core business in action

All organizations have a core product or service paid for by customers and which justifies their existence. If you have been hired to be part of this then knowing how it works will not be a problem. When you are not part of the core business it's important to accept that the only reason for your own job is to provide a service to the people who themselves provide services to the organization's customers. Understanding their concerns and passions will be essential for grasping why your own post exists and for knowing how to work alongside such colleagues. This is why you must see this product or service in action. When I worked at the BBC you were strongly encouraged, for instance, however humble your role, to visit a studio and see how programmes were made. If you had a senior role in a support department, at some point you would be pressed to do a little three-day production course where you found out at first hand that making programmes was not as easy as it looked. This was wise. Make sure you do the equivalent for whatever is the core business of your own new organization.

Trying to do the job too soon

This may seem strange because after all you have been appointed to get on and do the job. But in your first few weeks your task is to learn what the job really is rather than plunging into what you assume it is. The more responsible the role, the longer this period needs to be. So if you are a senior manager, your first three or four weeks should be spent listening, observing and asking questions. Useful questions for any role are

What are the main problems waiting to be solved here?

What can and should I be doing to solve them?

What do you expect from me?

228

What might be the one thing in relation to my job that would make your own job easier?

Believing that this job is just the same as your last job, only paid a bit more

This is a particular hazard if you have been promoted. A promotion is most unlikely to mean more of the same. The skills for which you were praised in your past job will most probably be taken for granted in the new one, and the new one may need skills that are significantly different. Here are some examples

Old Job	New Job
Focus on the detail	Focus on the bigger picture
Technical excellence	Managerial excellence
Operational skills	Leadership skills
Doing the job	Delegating the job
Taking instructions	Giving instructions

The solution is to get as clear as you can before you start, and then to clarify again exactly what the job needs. This may be different from what you have been led to believe, and may also differ from your personal fantasies of what you thought would be involved and can come as a shock. Typically, after the euphoria and excitement of the induction period, there is a sharp fall in confidence.

> I'd been in the job of team leader exactly six weeks. I went to a sales meeting where new targets were being discussed. The boss turned to me and asked me what 'intelligence' I'd gathered about likely trends in our market. I turned bright red. I hadn't gathered any 'intelligence'. I'd come expecting

229

just my own ideas to be what was wanted. Afterwards I realized I should have been spending time calling key customers, encouraging my team to do the same, consulting my team – all the obvious things. It had never occurred to me that so much of my attention should be focused outside the company. I went home that weekend with a serious crash in confidence and did actually consider resigning. The learning curve was steeper in that job than anything I'd ever experienced before. I hung on in there, but only just.

A candid conversation with your new boss

For some years I wrote an agony aunt column in a magazine where I replied to readers' career questions. Far and away the most common queries centred on the relationship with the boss and many such questions came down to one issue: how to get clear what the boss really wanted. Even with goodwill on both sides, there is often hesitancy to have the conversation that would be so helpful. Why? Hierarchy gets in the way – an exaggerated respect for seniority, a feeling on the part of the new person that the boss must be 'very busy': but what could be more important for a boss than to settle in a new member of their team? Embarrassment at appearing needy could possibly stop you asking for the clarity you deserve. Whatever the reasons, many people, bosses and new hires at all levels from the most senior to the most junior, neglect to do what is simple – a conversation on the first day, or at the very latest by the end of the first week where these questions are discussed and in detail:

What do you (boss) expect from me?

How will you know at the end of my first month whether I am doing OK? And then again at the end of my first three months, and year?

What immediate tasks are there for me to tackle?

What do I need to understand about this job in order to do it well?

230

What do I need to understand about the culture of the organization?

Where should I just get on with things and where do you need me to consult you first?

These are the safe areas because they are about the rational parts of the job. The area that few people indeed tackle is the whole question of the working relationship. Be brave: ask

How do you like to work with people who report to you? What kind of a working relationship should we expect to establish?

What really annoys you in a working relationship? What should I avoid at all costs?

What support and help can I expect from you while I'm in the early (or later) stages of learning how to do the job?

How will I get to know what you feel about my work? How honest will you be with me if you feel I'm getting it wrong?

Having heard answers to these questions then you can raise whatever you feel you need on your side – for instance some extra training, different equipment or office support.

Having this conversation was so important. I discovered that my new boss hated people sending him what he called 'alibi messages': emails that seemed to protect the sender's back. He also told me to think carefully before sending him long attachments to emails or copying him on issues that were not priorities for him and said that he never had regular one-to-one meetings. He told me that if I wanted to see him I should just approach his PA, get a date put in the diary and keep the meeting to 30 minutes, and that he would do the same with me. He disliked moaners. If I had a problem I should come to him with a suggested solution. For my part I was able to suggest that at the end of my first two weeks we should agree a meeting where he gave me frank feedback

231

> on how I was doing. I also alerted him to the idea that I was not impressed by the PA I had inherited and thought I should move her on as soon as possible and he agreed to this immediately. This was brilliant – it got us off to a good start.

You should assume that an important part of any job is managing upwards – that is managing your boss and other seniors. This whole idea can come as a surprise to people who think of management as being invariably about managing downwards. But actually, managing upwards skilfully is just as important. To do this well, you also need to stop thinking about your boss as just a work machine. Get to know him or her as a whole person. Show an interest in their home life; take the trouble to see what problems they face and how the world looks from their perspective. When you do this you create an ally in your manager rather than seeing them as someone to be feared and kept at bay.

Finding friends

If the organization has allocated you a buddy for your induction then be grateful and pump them for information. Even if you do have this official friend, you should make it part of your first few weeks to find others. Take time to get to know people: ask them about their work, their home lives and other matters that preoccupy them. Suggest a quick drink after work if it seems there is something in common. And make the first move rather than hanging back, waiting to be asked. Building a network of friends will help in many ways: you will understand the new organization and job in more depth and more quickly. You will feel more in control. It will help you feel you really belong rather than lingering around the edges as an outsider, and most crucially it will provide the beginnings of an informal support and counselling network – something everyone needs to do their jobs well.

232

Early wins

Whatever the level of job, it will help to have some early wins. You will feel pride in achievements that matter to the organization and your reputation as a problem solver will grow. The best early wins will typically have these features:

They are associated with issues that have been left unresolved for some time and have been a cause for frustration all round

They cost little money and no massive investment of time to implement

They have a big impact

You see how to resolve them because you are looking at them afresh, without all the limiting assumptions that everyone else has been making

They send an important message about your style of working, values and commitments

Here are some examples:

Elli set up a new method of planning the duty rota for the group of GPs where she had become practice manager. It only took her a day to work out how to do it and had enormous positive impact on the way the whole health centre ran.

Kath made a successful case for buying a reasonably priced drinks-making system to provide free coffee and tea for the team in which she was working, thus solving long-standing grumbles about the expense and inconvenience of having to leave the building to buy coffee at local sandwich bars and coffee shops.

Alastair introduced a simple and effective new method of logging and relaying messages for the two senior journalists to whom he was PA, thus instantly improving the efficiency of their work.

233

Kenny insisted on re-grading the secretaries in his team, negotiating new titles and enhanced salaries that more fairly and accurately reflected their responsibilities.

Brooke swiftly agreed to getting business cards printed for a group of people who had previously been considered too junior to have them. The increase in their morale and in their regard for her was palpable.

Marsha announced her commitment to banishing the punitive culture she could see in her department. When one of her senior team flagrantly and rudely refused to cooperate, this man was dismissed.

Starting a new job is one of life's major transitions. Treat it with the attention it deserves and you will find that all your work in preparing and then going through the selection process has paid off magnificently.